John Norwood's Railroads

Edited by Debra K. McMillin

Library of Congress Catalog Card Number: 94-72883
ISBN: 0-911581-31-6

First Edition
Printed in the United States of America

Heimburger House Publishing Company
7236 West Madison
Forest Park, IL 60130

Dedication

This book is dedicated to the two progenitors of the tens of thousands of avid and dedicated modern railfans who keep fires of love and memories of the days of steam railroads burning brightly.

The first is George A. Crofutt who wrote the first railfan book in 1881: *Crofutt's Grip-Sack Guide of Colorado*. (A second *Grip-Sack Guide of Colorado* followed in 1885).

Crofutt religiously followed the progress of railroad construction in Colorado and rode each new section. In many instances, he utilized stagecoaches and rode horseback to travel from one rail's end to another. He chronicled each rail or stage route in the state of Colorado, and his narratives and accounts cover in detail railroad stations, schedules, fares and train accommodations. The names of towns and information about them that he included is all-embracing.

The second man to whom I dedicate this book is William H. Jackson, one of the foremost photographers of the era. He took almost as many pictures of the railroads under construction and operation as photojournalists of *Life* magazine have taken for that publication. His production, coverage and quality are so extraordinary that they seem impossible.

An engine is positioned on the girder beams of Hanging Bridge on the Arkansas River before the suspension beams are in place. *W.H. Jackson, Colorado State Historical Society*

4

Contents

Foreword

I retired early for one reason: I had a surfeit of railroading. I never wanted to ever again see, hear, smell or think about a railroad. For three years I was able to maintain this attitude, but then I began suffering from a different surfeit or, more accurately, two of them: I was tired of traveling and bored to death with leisure time. Therefore, I started a second career as an independent railroad consultant.

The year 1965 marked the beginning of an emerging interest in the Silverton Branch by railfans. This interest just kept increasing. Those of us who earned our bread and butter on the railroad could hardly understand why anybody with good sense would pay money to ride a train over a piece of railroad like the 47 miles from Durango, Colorado to Silverton. We thought that they must be old-timers who, just for the nostalgia, wanted to make one last trip down memory lane. But these people were not old-timers. They were young people or middle-aged at most.

ENIGMATIC 'RAILNUTS'

They were not just railfans: they were "railnuts." They have not changed much over the years, either, except that now they cover more territory. They flock to any place where a steam-powered railroad has been resurrected. Their numbers continuously grow, too, so that now they number in the tens of thousands. They ride trains, build railroad models, organize clubs, buy souvenirs—and they buy railroad books and magazines.

Remembrance need not come from things that have happened to us personally. It can derive from history. Sometimes history has been so vivid that it seems we have been a part of it; history needs distance and perspective to become part of us. It is a voice forever sounding across the ages and we read it according to our prejudices and associations. I relive history in pictures inspired by Conrad, Stevenson and London of sails billowing under tropical skies off a Pacific island paradise replete with palm trees, grass shacks and tawny maidens. Railfans, of course, relive history in pictures of sleek high-wheeled steam engines, whose gleaming varnish and shining rails lead to the horizon, of the staccato bark of perfectly tuned valves bouncing from the walls of a railside cliff, or of a spiral of coal smoke trailing from the stack.

Thus, it remains that remembrance, either personal or secondhand, is the only paradise out of which we cannot be driven away.

My wish is that each of us forever be given our own imagined paradises. For railfans, I wish blustering smoke from a stack, cinders in the eye, hands on the throttle and drivers churning. For myself, I'll take the South Seas, although, with my years, I do not know what I would do with the tawny maidens.

An artist depicts the water tank at Deer Creek Canyon on the Denver, South Park and Pacific. *Colorado Historical Society*

Heavyweight steam train reminiscent of the 1930s and 1940s. *Norm Schreiner collection*

Chapter 1

Mears' Quest for Ouray

In June of 1889 Otto Mears was forced to admit that it was physically impossible to complete the Silverton Railroad from Silverton to Ouray over Red Mountain. This recognition, however, only made him determined to get to Ouray. As a result, he had his engineers lay out a route from Durango via Dolores, Lizard Head Pass and Dallas Divide. June of 1890 drew 1,500 workmen to the task of building the Rio Grande Southern. The line was built with operations going forward simultaneously from Ridgway and Durango, Colorado.

On December 20, 1891, 11 miles south of Rico, Mears drove the traditional golden spike to tie the two segments together. The next day the first through train out of Durango started west. Scheduled service was soon in effect involving a night layover at Rico to cover the 162 miles of what is, without a doubt, the longest shoofly ever built for a railroad. The word "shoofly" was brought into use during the Civil War by military railroad men who used the French military term "shouffle" to describe the tactic of quickly building a road around an enemy strong point to act as a detour and permit investment of areas beyond the strong point.

SURMOUNTING LIZARD HEAD

Otto Mears never got to Ouray, but he did get to Ridgway, only 10.33 miles from Ouray, which the Denver & Rio Grande had reached from Montrose. To accomplish this feat, Mears built over Lizard Head Pass at an elevation of 10,222 feet. This was 207 feet higher than D&RG's Cumbres Pass and 634 feet lower than its Marshall Pass crossing.

At an elevation of 10,222 feet, Lizard Head Pass is 2,934 feet lower than Lizard Head Peak, the unusual peak shaped like a lizard's head and said to be the toughest mountain climb in Colorado. It was first climbed in 1920 by Albert Ellingwood. An Indian/trapper trail is known to have been in use over this pass as early as 1833. A wagon road came into use in 1870, and 20 years later Mears laid rails there.

There was a small, short-lived town in the pass, as well as considerable railroad structures including a lot of snow fences, a covered wye and sta-

tion buildings. Information about the structure is minimal, but it is said to have been an exact copy of the one in Corkscrew Gulch on the Silverton Railroad, the line Mears was unable to complete from Silverton to Ouray.

It is difficult to imagine when crossing Lizard Head Pass by automobile on Colorado Highway #145, that railroad operation was so hellish during the winters; however, the existence of so much covered trackage, and the stories of it being necessary to keep snow plows in almost constant use paints a picture that must be believed.

Rio Grande Southern Engine No. 41 sits on a side track at Ridgway in the spring of 1950. Her paint is getting dirty. This locomotive was later restored and now runs at Knott's Berry Farm in California. *M.D. McCarter collection*

8

The date is March 29, 1950. Rio Grande Southern Engine No. 455 pulls a freight train up Dallas Divide while the fireman steadily pours coal to her. *M.D. McCarter collection*

Rio Grande Engine No. 452 approaches Dallas Divide with a Rio Grande Southern freight train in tow. The year is 1949. *M.D. McCarter collection*

Rio Grande Southern Engine No. 461 makes a pickup at Lizard Head in September, 1951. *Colorado State Historical Society*

This silver pass, issued to Denver & Rio Grande General Passenger Agent F.A. Wadleigh in 1892 by Otto Mears' Silverton Railroad, was good on the Silverton Railroad and the Rio Grande Southern Railroad. *Colorado State Historical Society*

These four Rio Grande Southern passes were issued to Henry Swan, a trustee of the Denver & Rio Grande Western Railroad, by RGS receivers. *Colorado State Historical Society*

Mears Hires Photographer Jackson

In 1895 Otto Mears became impressed with the use the Denver & Rio Grande was making of William H. Jackson's photos for advertising purposes, and arrangements were made for him to take photos on the Rio Grande Southern. Jackson's assigned car, D&RG business car *K*, was coupled to RGS car *Rico* and given RGS Engine #1 for power. This engine, a 2-8-0, was the first engine on the RGS.

For a railroad of its size, the RGS had an exceptional number of business cars that were used on Mears' various lines. The D&RG, however, was relatively as well supplied. Palmer used the alphabet to identify D&RG business cars, and he eventually reached the letter R. As both railroads matured and there was less use for so many business cars, they were put to various other uses.

Careful study of the picture to the right shows that D&RG car *K* is still equipped with link- and-pin couplings. Soon after the Civil War, railroads began experimenting with ideas of an automatic coupler. In the last decade of the 1800s, two or three designs evolved that resemble our modern automatic couplers. Conversion from link-and-pin couplings to automatic couplings presented an almost insurmountable problem, however, while both concepts were in use on ore cars that had to be kept working. Expedients were worked out, including a coupler pocket that could accept either a link or coupler head. The D&RG and, presumably, the RGS and Rio Grande Western, began conversion about 1900 and had the program well under way by 1903-04. The Interstate Commerce Commission finally set 1908 as the date when cars could not be interchanged unless equipped with automatic couplers.

By 1903-04 many of the narrow gauge cars in use were approaching obsolescence because of hard usage or outdated capacity or design. At the time, it cost about $50 per car to make a conversion, a considerable amount then. Many cars were not considered worth this and consequently were scrapped.

W.H. Jackson took this picture of Rio Grande Southern Engine No. 20 pulling a caboose, two passenger cars and a gondola. It is unusual to *see* a train carrying two white flags — one on the locomotive and one on the rear car. The flag on the engine means that this is a special, unscheduled train. *W.H. Jackson/Colorado State Historical Society*

Rio Grande Southern Engine No. 1, pulling RGS business car *Rico* and Denver & Rio Grande business car *K*, approaches the Mancos-La Plata Divide preparatory to taking water in 1895. Ahead of this train, being run for the express purpose of letting William H. Jackson take publicity pictures for Mears' RGS, is a double-header freight train chugging around the loop at Mancos-La Plata Divide and just approaching the summit.

On this tour, Jackson made many outstanding photographs of scenic marvels on the RGS, including scenes and structures in the Ophir Loop area and at Lizard Head Pass. At the time that Mears employed him, William H. Jackson had achieved a reputation as the foremost photographer of Western scenes, especially of railroad scenes. The D&RG, Union Pacific and other Rocky Mountain area lines kept him constantly occupied. *Colorado State Historical Society*

ABOVE: W.H. Jackson took this great panoramic view of Ophir Loop (directly below), including several trestles, for the Rio Grande Southern. W.H. Jackson/Colorado State Historical Society

LEFT: RGS Engine No. 1 pulls RGS business car *Rico* and D&RG business car *K* on Lizard Head Pass. Note the link-and-pin coupling on the rear of car *K*. *W.H. Jackson/Colorado State Historical Society*

A Rio Grande Southern passenger train arrives at Hesperus, Colorado while a mixed train sits on the siding. The train order board indicates an order to deliver. *Colorado State Historical Society*

Train Time

It's train time at Hesperus, Colorado. Judging from the radiator shape of the automobile, it is probably in the early 1920s. In the spring of 1920 my father had just resigned from the Rio Grande Southern as an agent/telegrapher to return to the South. As a final holiday in the West, he took the family on a trip to Mesa Verde. The trip was made in Oldsmobiles, owned by the tour company, that resembled the one in this picture. The arrival of the daily passenger trains at Hesperus while we lived there produced the scene I was later to see in many small towns on the numerous railroads my father worked for before ending his career as boomer telegrapher.

Early in the day, farmers began to arrive in town with full cream cans to be checked by baggage to the nearest creamery which bought the area's cream. They would also pick up their empty cream cans (creameries furnished the cans with brass tags identifying the farmers they belonged to). The farmers and their families then went shopping or visiting and returned to the depot in time to see the passenger train arrive. The next arrival would be a dray with a traveling salesman's trunk of wares to be checked along with the traveling trunks of passengers planning trips requiring more clothes than one suitcase could hold. Customers with outgoing Railway

This Rio Grande Southern passenger train is picking up passengers at Mancos, Colorado. Except for the tower above the bay window, the Mancos and Hesperus, Colorado railroad stations looked exactly alike. Our family lived above this depot in 1920 when my father was an agent for the RGS. *Colorado State Historical Society*

Express shipments came in frequently as did those checking ticket information. If the weather was hot, inclement, or if it was the dead of winter, the waiting room would be crowded with waiting passengers or people meeting incoming family or friends.

Outside on the platform, the tobacco chewers congregated, and the men and boys engaged in telling "dirty" stories. They would sit or lean on empty baggage trucks, so the student telegrapher or station helper had to run them off to load cream, express and baggage for the expected train. He loaded the cargo on the trucks and then spotted them at locations he knew would be properly spaced for the train's usual make up. The mail truck came first because the mail car was always behind the engine; then came the truck for the express and baggage car. It was a wonder to see how the engineer always stopped the train's cars in exactly the correct spots.

TRAIN ORDERS

Inside the office, a harried agent copied last minute train orders and obtained a clearance card, while late arriving passengers hurried to buy tickets and check their baggage. In the picture here, for instance, the Swift-type train order signal is in a position indicating that there are train orders for delivery.

The train on the adjacent tracks in the picture could be a mixed train, meaning it has a consist of both passenger cars and freight cars, or it could be a freight train hauling a deadhead passenger car.

About a mile from town, the engineman whistled for the station: one prolonged blast. The populace then flowed out of the waiting room, as well as from Main Street, to enjoy one half of the day's excitement. The other half was enjoyed when the train from the opposite direction arrived. When the RGS, or any other railroad, operated more passenger trains than one eastbound and one westbound train per day, the populace was living in clover. Each train had to be met whether work got done or not.

OLD D&RG PHOTO

There are intriguing anomalies in the photograph on page 17. The automobile is of a vintage 1920-25. On the box car on the adjacent track the car number is freshly stenciled, but the ownership in the upper left-hand corner still reads Denver & Rio Grande, indicating that the D&RG has not yet gotten around to restenciling rolling stock that has just been chartered.

My Stint at the RGS

When I was loaned to the Rio Grande Southern by the Denver & Rio Grande in 1942 to go to Durango and work as a train dispatcher, among other duties defined to me later, I soon learned two things: the Galloping Geese were the hottest thing on the RGS, and Placerville was one of the most important stations on the line.

LADY TELEGRAPHER

Placerville was manned by an old-time lady Morse telegrapher, and I had orders not to do anything that would anger her to the point of quitting. In the end, the greatest surprise of all was that this lady operator/agent was a hell of a fine old gal. She set up and thoroughly enjoyed creating situations that would make C.W. Graebing and R.R. Boucher, the operating heads of the RGS, squirm.

I made them squirm even more when I insisted on being paid Denver & Rio Grande scale for a dispatcher. They were still arguing about it when I left, but I did get paid the salary, plus expenses. I later learned just how badly strapped the RGS was, and that these two men were taking only $100 per month each as salaries.

CRAMMED IN AT PLACERVILLE

The location of the RGS Placerville depot and tracks was far from ideal, but Mears, unlike General Palmer, did not believe in disrupting the community. Placerville was already a bustling town when he reached it, so he made the best of a bad location. The available ground was hemmed at the back by a steep, rocky hillside and in the front by the San Miguel River. A fill of rock and dirt with some log cribbing permitted a main track and a side track to run in front of the depot which was used as a team track and a holding track to store RGS equipment, including the old RGS rotary snowplow, which sat long unused.

As the name implies, the community of Placerville resulted from the discovery of placer gold in the vicinity by prospectors coming in from Silverton. The arrival of the RGS gave the almost-ghost town a second life, and some lumbering developed. The greatest boost came from a burgeoning cattle population. Sheep followed later, and Placerville became one of the major stock loading stations on the RGS. The other was Dolores, Colorado. The stockyards were located near Placerville, where space was available, and had the capacity to handle and load 30 cars for one train. The Dolores stockyards had the same capacity.

SAN MIGUEL FLOOD

The San Miguel River was the primary reason I was on the RGS. It had gone on a rampage from heavy rains, and the tracks and depot at Placerville were almost lost. At the same time, the

Dolores River was flooding, and all the tributaries were running full. The mountain meadows that the RGS traversed at some places were saturated. A lot of track was lost or impassable.

The stock season was on, however, and we kept trying to run empties in and haul livestock out. It finally became hopeless when a double-header train of stock loaded at Placerville reached Leopard Creek, 16 miles from Ridgway. While traveling cautiously across the saturated roadbed, Engine #456 quit moving. It was not derailed; it

Galloping Goose No. 4 sits at Placerville on May 29, 1949. Behind it, RGS Engine No. 74 hauls a mixed train. The old RGS rotary snowplow (center) sits on a back track. These tracks were once almost lost due to high water on the San Miguel River. Much other track was lost or damaged during the flood. *Colorado State Historical Society*

simply sank through the rotting ties laying on top of the soupy mud, and it just kept sinking. The second engine soon began to follow suit.

When daylight came, the cattle were unloaded and driven to Ridgway to be loaded out in Denver & Rio Grande cars and forwarded.

Placerville is 25 miles from Ridgway via State Highway #62. It is 27 miles by the old RGS grade. Railbuffs can still go there easily, stand on the banks of the San Miguel and dream of the days when Placerville was an important station on

a now long gone railroad — a line built by Otto Mears to prove that if he could not go over a mountain to Ouray, he could go around it — and remember the Galloping Geese that were scheduled as First Class trains.

CREATING THE GEESE

In 1930 the RGS deficit approached $3 million, and the railroad was going in the hole at the rate of $56,000 each year. It went into receivership, and Victor A. Miller was appointed receiver.

Rio Grande Southern Engine No. 461 pulls an RGS double deck stock car and other miscellaneous cars.
Dr. Richard Severance

One of his first moves was to discontinue all steam engine passenger service. In lieu of this type of service, Jack Odenbaugh, chief mechanic, fashioned seven railbuses and quickly dubbed them the Galloping Geese. They were powered with Winston or Pierce Arrow motors. The color scheme was overall silvery. In the tonneau of the power unit, seven passengers and the driver could ride fairly comfortably. A trailing unit handled the less than carload freight, mail and express. The ride was not quite as comfortable when as many as 10 or even a dozen passengers were crowded into the tonneau, especially if part of them were Indians or sheepherders just coming in fresh from a long stay with sheep.

The Galloping Geese were operated on a timetable schedule, carried the designation of First Class, and all trains cleared for them. The first time I looked out of my office window, located on the second story of the Rio Grande depot at Durango, and saw a Goose, I could not believe my eyes.

Goose #4, pictured here, was one of six Geese remaining at this time from a fleet of seven. One Goose had ceased to exist in an accident near Hesperus, Colorado.

In the two months that I was on the RGS, I never stopped marveling at the ingenuity and dedication it took for the drivers to get over the road.

I quickly learned not to worry when one of the Geese was overdue at a reporting point. Eventually, they always showed. Each driver carried a box of tools. The basic tools were a heavy wire cutter and a pair of pliers. Many ranchers lost barbed wire from their fences purloined by drivers needing wire to tie up dragging cowcatchers, brake shoes, etc. If they derailed, they simply conscripted the help of any male, and sometimes a few female passengers, and rerailed the unit.

I will always fondly remember my stint on the RGS in 1942. There are not many people left who can brag that they dispatched the Galloping Geese.

Here we see Rio Grande Southern Engine No. 20 at a later date than the photo below. The elk horns and locomotive's name are gone and a straight stack has replaced the diamond stack. The engine is carrying white flags denoting that she has orders and has been cleared to run as an extra, unscheduled train. *Colorado State Historical Society*

Rio Grande Southern Engine No. 20, the *Emma Sweeny*, still has her diamond stack in this photograph and is all spruced up with elk horns and a coal oil headlight. *Colorado State Historical Society*

BELOW: Rio Grande Southern Engine No. 455 and No. 464 (behind) sit side by side on a spring afternoon. Both locomotives are still equipped with snowplows. *Colorado State Historical Society*

RGS Clean-Up Train

In August of 1952, John Krause, a dedicated fan and photographer of the Denver & Rio Grande Western and the Rio Grande Southern, followed a train powered by RGS Engine #461 from Ridgway to Durango, Colorado as it cleaned the RGS line of cars and some equipment because of the dismantling of the 3-foot gauge railroad. The Rio Grande Southern was the first to go; the Denver & Rio Grande Western would follow a little more than a decade later.

To fully appreciate the story of what this abandonment entailed, and why many railfans felt they were losing a monument to the opening of the West and Colorado's mountain ranges, something must be told of the history of Otto Mear's 162-mile-long shoofly.

THREE RAIL LINES

Otto Mears built and operated three short railroads out of Silverton, Colorado that connected with the Rio Grande at that point. Mears tried to build one of these, the Silverton Railroad, over Red Mountain and into Ouray, Colorado. Unsuc-cessful in this attempt, he built the RGS around the mountain through terrain almost as impregnable as that of the Silverton Northern. Between 1867 and 1886, he built a dozen toll wagon roads in the southwestern mountains of Colorado, and no one obstacle was going to keep him from going where he wanted. He built the Rio Grande Southern, the railroad that was overwhelmingly improbable.

A 27-mile wagon toll road of Mears' was already in use between Ridgway and Telluride over Dallas Divide that could be used as grade for the railroad. There was a D&RG survey for an extension of the D&RG from Durango to Mancos. The D&RG could not make up its mind to build it; Mears made up his mind quickly to use the proposed route.

Mears incorporated the RGS in 1889 and, at the same time, incorporated the Rio Grande Southern Construction Company. Both were Mears', and the engineers who headed the construction company were the same ones who had built Mears' three Silverton short lines.

The cleanup train sends a signal of distress into a calm atmosphere of a clear Colorado sky. Smoke such as this comes only when the fireman is doing a poor job of stoking. However, the fire is good enough to get a plume of steam from the pop off valve. The water tank is about to collapse and the bands have loosened. Apparently it has been leaking long enough to have produced a puddle where cattails have started to grow. *Dr. Richard Severance*

LEFT: RGS Engine No. 461, August, 1952, is being readied at Ridgway to start a trip toward Durango to pick up cars that are going to be scrapped or returned to the D&RGW if there are any of such ownership left on line and not yet removed. Note the weeds, tall grass and overall aspect of a once proud installation of a roundhouse and facilities gone to wrack and ruin. Visible just over the wing of the wedge plow is the enclosed track car used by Roadmaster R.M. Murray for riding the line on inspections when the road was still operating. The cars in sight will be scrapped where they sit.

Sometime in the past when the RGS was still a viable railroad operating under the rules, Engine No. 461 was apparently run as an unscheduled train, an extra, and displayed white signals to denote it was doing so by train order authority. That could have been as far back as December, 1951. Now on the date the present train is to be run it will require neither train order authority or signal flags. Nevertheless, there is one dirty, weathered flag in place and the two lamp signals are still in place. The last engine crew was probably too discouraged to bother with removing them. *Dr. Richard Severance*

The line-clearing cleanup train with RGS Engine No. 461 on the point followed by RGS No. 7409, an empty single deck stock car and RGS Caboose No. 0400 has just left Ridgway and is about to cross Highway 62. It is August, 1952. *Dr. Richard Severance*

Construction was started at both ends of the proposed line, Ridgway and Durango. As quickly as the track from Durango reached the Porter Coal mines, five miles west of Durango, the RGS began hauling coal. Scheduled trains began operating out of Ridgway to Telluride, 45 miles away, when track was completed on this section. The same was done out of Durango when the track was in place to Mancos.

The two ends met in December, 1891, about 11 miles south of Rico. The first through train was run in December 21, 1891. It took two days for the trip. An overnight stop was made at Rico until finally there was overnight service with the addition of Pullman cars to the trains. The Pullman berths were not "coeducational." Mears insisted only one person in a bunk at a time. Anyway, the bunks were too narrow to be occupied comfortably by more than a single individual.

INTO BANKRUPTCY

In 1893, two years after the RGS was completed, the silver panic hit. The railroad went into bankruptcy, and the Denver & Rio Grande was named receiver. Under receivership, the start-up bonds amounting to $4.5 million were not defaulted, and interest was paid regularly until 1922. But in all the years the RGS existed, it never paid a dividend. The D&RGW returned the road to the RGS in 1922.

The fireboy has cleaned up his firing act and RGS Engine No. 461 crosses Highway 62 just out of Ridgway with its consist of RGS Caboose No. 0400 and RGS Stock Car No. 7409. No. 7409 is in better shape than those left at Ridgway to be scrapped. It may be intended for setting out somewhere along the line for the dismantling crew to load O.T.M. (other track material) scrap to go out on a later train. *Dr. Richard Severance*

Under receivership, the plant was kept operational but the D&RG had taken advantage of all means within the law to benefit itself. Exorbitant amounts were charged for supplies, track and structure maintenance. The bankrupt line carried a heavy payroll, top heavy with D&RG management personnel. As much as possible hand-me-down material and equipment was supplied at almost new prices. RGS locomotives and rolling stock was allowed to set idle awaiting repairs, or blatantly ignored while D&RG equipment was used. Of course, the RGS was billed heavily for its use.

There was enough ore, lumber and livestock moving, and a U.S. mail contract so that trains kept running and operations continued, but never in the black. In 1935, the Manhattan Project brought a burst of action. It was not until the first atom bomb exploded that anyone knew there was such a thing. Freight trains were running rather frequently, and it was not quite as difficult to meet the payroll and to make some improvements to the track and engines.

Ore dumps at old mines had been formed when mines discarded a reddish deposit that was thought to be of no value. These dumps were reclaimed as new sources of the material were sought and developed. Vanadium, only a nuisance to the Rico-Dolores-Telluride-area mines, was a source for uranium, and at Los Alamos and Oak Ridge the atom bomb was being secretly developed. A railroad operating on faith and mountain air to stay alive was suddenly and unknowingly carrying the hottest commodity in railroad history under an impenetrable cloak of secrecy.

It was too good to last, and it did not. Soon it was back to worrying about how to meet the next payroll or how to obtain enough coal on credit to

RGS Engine No. 461 has successfully come about three miles from Ridgway. It still has only RGS No. 7409, an empty stock car, and RGS Caboose No. 0400 in tow. *Dr. Richard Severance*

keep the engines hauling cars. The terminal costs at both Durango and Ridgway owed to the D&RGW pyramided month by month, although the Grande was not pushing for payment. After all, a pot cannot call a kettle black. It was not until April 11, 1947 that the Rio Grande emerged from 12 years of bankruptcy and trusteeship.

ABANDONMENT LOOMS

As the 1950s approached it was apparent the RGS could not survive. Applications made for abandonment were unsuccessful due to strong pressure from counties involved and political pressure from other sources. All the counties forgave their tax claims, and employees made concessions involving wage scales. The Reconstruction Finance Commission put up $65,000 to make some absolutely necessary track and bridge repairs. It also paid some debts for fuel and overdue employee wages.

The battle was a stalemate, and in 1951 the Rio Grande Southern Railroad folded.

During the final decade of operations, only by the grace of God and a plentiful supply of baling wire were engines kept hauling and cars rolling on a track structure constantly deteriorating. Of course, there were frequent derailments and equipment malfunctions. The two top operating men could not easily be designated by titles. C.W. Graebing directed operations, and Roy Boucher handled the secretarial and treasurer functions. Cass M. Herrington became the receiver in 1939 and remained as such until about the end of the 1940s. Pierpont Fuller, Jr. was the last receiver on the RGS. Johnny Helms was elevated into the chief dispatcher's chair from a telegrapher job. After the RGS folded he came to work for the Denver & Rio Grande Western as a train dispatcher. R.M. Murray, of the track and structures department, was boss of about 10 or 12 section men. They all worked their hearts out and existed on starvation wages to keep the line going. Theirs was not an enviable position.

TAKE IT CALMLY

When a train was started on a run, the crew at headquarters just learned to wait as calmly as possible until it either arrived at a tie-up or got word of troubles ahead. Minor derailments or malfunctions were taken care of by the men with the train. More serious ones were reported as quickly as possible when a crew member could walk out to a ranch or a town where a phone was available. There was a phone at the Lizard Head snow shed, but it was seldom operable.

The burden of debts as of September 30, 1951 was placed as being almost $10 million. This included nearly $1 million for back wages, county taxes, unemployment and Railroad Retirement pension payments.

The last train hauling revenue business ran from Rico to Ridgway in December, 1951. Engine #461, on the head end, was the last RGS locomotive used in revenue service.

The contract dismantlers used RGS Engine #461 with an auxiliary water car and a passenger car for an office until the end of the dismantling job. It was the last operating RGS locomotive to bear the Rio Grande Southern insignia. Engine #461 was dismantled in 1953. D&RGW Engine #452 was the last locomotive to power a train on the RGS. It pulled the last train of scrap and OTM (other track material) resulting from the dismantling.

The clean-up train using RGS Engine #461, followed, recorded and photographed by John Krause, was the last one pulling cars destined for scrap or delivery back to the D&RGW in case of leased, loaned or interchanged cars.

RGS Engine No. 461 holds on to the stock car it had out of Ridgway, RGS No. 7409, and picks up another empty RGS stock car that will end up being scrapped. It is August, 1952 but note how in only one summer of disuse, Nature is already beginning to heal the scar of the roadbed with tall grass. The smoke plume still rises almost vertically. *Dr. Richard Severance*

RGS Engine No. 461 has made it over the hump and picked up a string of miscellaneous cars headed for the bone yard. The lumber from the deserted station buildings will soon be salvaged by residents of the area to construct ranch buildings, maybe even a house. Then there will be only open space except for the one structure that is the last to fade away in any ghost town, a privy. *Dr. Richard Severance*

The cleanup train is approaching Dallas Divide; Engine RGS No. 461 and the first three cars behind it are on level track. The balance of cars that have been picked up enroute are not quite over the hump. That fireman is still sending billows of coal smoke into the clean mountain air, but there is now a breeze causing it to trail back over the train. *Dr. Richard Severance*

The cleanup train has just picked up another car and caboose No. 0400 is still obstructing part of a dirt ranch road that leads to some ranch buildings that are in as badly deteriorated condition as the railroad. The Rio Grande converted a number of old standard gauge box cars to narrow gauge flat cars to handle the Farmington pipe movement. *Dr. Richard Severance*

The cleanup train has about completed its assignment and stops at one of the few water tanks that still can supply water. So many had been allowed to dry out after it became certain that operations would cease that they would not hold water when the dismantling project began in 1952. For that reason the contractor kept an auxiliary water car coupled to the engine when using RGS Engine No. 461. *Dr. Richard Severance*

RGS Engine No. 461 with an increased consist rolls up toward the Dallas Divide. A wind is blowing the black cloud into the sky partly obscuring the natural clouds.

The signal flags seen just to the left of the rear of the stock car marks a survey point on a mapping project the Bureau of Land Management is engaged in.
Dr. Richard Severance

ABOVE LEFT: Just drifting along the water level grade paralleling the San Miguel River RGS Engine No. 461 and its string of cleanup cars approaches the Placerville depot. *Dr. Richard Severance*

33

Chapter 2
Colorado & Southern
Narrow Gauge

The Infamous Scale Test Car

This test car sitting on the Colorado & Southern tracks at Leadville, waiting to go to Climax to test scales, was the source of many headaches for the Denver & Rio Grande and, most likely, other railroads.

As a member of the Western Weighing & Inspection Bureau, we had to furnish a scale inspector and mechanic annually to test all railroad-connected scales on the system for accuracy. If I were asked what single piece of equipment we most dreaded to see lined up to move, I could

answer without hesitation: the scale test car.

The scale inspector had a heavy schedule, and it was not always practical to hold up movement waiting for a slow train, so we had to line the test car behind the caboose of the train and restrict it to a maximum of 25 mph while it was being handled.

The pressure eased when we quit handling livestock, removed all of our stockyards and their scales, and went to carload rates on many of our mine products.

Western Weighing & Inspection Bureau's Scale Test Car No. 910 hooked behind this caboose meant this train was restricted to a 25 mph maximum. *Denver Public Library*

Form 31 Train Orders

This standard railroad train order Form 31 is on a Colorado & Southern Form 2415. Form 31 train orders were issued when it was imperative to confirm that delivery had been made to a train. The train receiving the copy had to be brought to a stop, and the conductor had to go into the train order office to receive his copy. While he was there, he had to read the order back to the operator and sign for receipt. The operator could not ask for a clearance card listing this order until the conductor had read and signed for it.

We can tell by the handwriting that the operator who copied this order was not one of the old boomer operators who wrote in their own distinctive, flowing manner. Also, it was against the rules to interline (notice that the word "cut" is interlined after the word "tunnel"). The date was supposed to have the month written out, and the year has been overlined to 1901.

It is intriguing to imagine that this order was issued in connection with the snowslide in the lower photo.

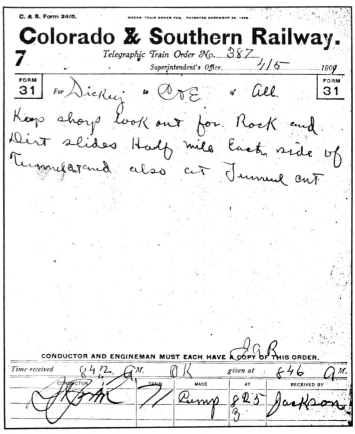

Colorado & Southern train orders. *Don Heimburger collection*

This cut was made through a snowslide on the Colorado & Southern Railroad around 1901. Judging from the terrain, it appears to be on the Leadville-Dillon portion of the Blue River Branch of the Denver & Rio Grande Western while it was under lease to the Colorado & Southern. *Denver Public Library*

35

Blue River Branch

Colorado & Southern Engine #69 is at Leadville, Colorado. The Leadville roundhouse was square, and the period is around the time that the C&S was leasing and operating the Blue River Branch of the Denver & Rio Grande, a narrow gauge operation.

The D&RG built the 35.68-mile Blue River Branch from Leadville to Dillon in 1881-82. Its operation ceased in 1909, but rails were not pulled up until 1924. For a period after 1909, the C&S leased and operated the line.

As superintendent of the Colorado division, and later as an incumbent of several general office assignments, I had the chance to become familiar with the area and the C&S operation between Leadville and Climax, which was standard gauge by that time.

Colorado & Southern Engine No. 69 sits at Leadville's square roundhouse. *Denver Public Library*

Twenty-three miles from Denver, a C&S passenger train rounds Inspiration Point in Clear Creek Canyon. Note that a large number of the ties that were hacked to length instead of being sawed off are still in the track. *Denver Public Library*

One Too Many

This shot of an eastbound Colorado & Southern passenger train rounding Inspiration Point in Clear Creek Canyon, 23 miles from Denver, has been used many times by Rocky Mountain railroad authors. These tracks, which had previously belonged to the Colorado Central and the Denver South Park & Pacific, were acquired by the C&S from the DSP&P. Highway #6 now runs along Clear Creek at this location.

Many of the scenes photographed in Colorado tend to appear similar to other locations. For instance, this scene could just as well have been shot on the Silverton Branch, the Black Canyon or the Royal Gorge. This effect is true of both mountains and canyons. I first realized this several years ago when I gave a slide show of Colorado mountains and scenery following a festive dinner. My slides were nicely arranged, indexed and cata-

logued (but not numbered) in a tray holding over 500 slides. This was before magazine-type slide projectors were common.

Because I did not want to be a wet blanket during the dinner, I had imbibed drink for drink with the rest of the gathering. When I arose from my seat to adjust the screen about midway through the show, one of my feet caught in the projector's cord, the cord caught on the tray and slides piled up all over the floor.

Later, when I tried to replace the slides in the trays, I discovered that I had developed a habit of snapping all my shots of peaks when there was a cloud showing above them and that, for this reason, all the peaks looked alike. Twenty plus years later those slides still have not been sorted out!

37

This is the White Pass & Yukon Railroad's second Engine No. 4. This 2-6-2 was built by Baldwin in April, 1912 for the Klondike Mines Railway and was sold to the WP&Y in 1942. It was eventually shipped to Wisconsin for use on tourist lines in the Midwest and on the East Coast. It was last in service on the Petticoat Junction Railroad in Sevierville, Tennessee. *M.D. McCarter collection*

Chapter 3
Three Notable Narrow Gauge Lines

White Pass & Yukon Railroad

Gold was discovered on the beaches of Juneau, Alaska in 1880, but this failed to touch off an explosive rush to the field. Then, in 1896, George Carmack and his Indian partner made a strike on Rabbit Creek, a tributary of the Klondike River. Other prospectors in the Klondike Region also made discoveries, especially on Bonanza Creek, another tributary of the Klondike River.

In the late fall of 1897, a group of miners returning from the Yukon Valley arrived at Seattle with approximately one and one half tons of gold between them. The news quickly spread all over the United States, Canada and other countries, and the Klondike Rush of 1897-98 was triggered. By the spring of 1898, the Canadian police had cleared 30,000 people through the checkpoint at White Pass, located on the boundaries between Alaska and Canada.

Many more prospectors had left their bones along the trail between Skagway and the checkpoint. Also, about 3,000 horses perished on the perilous Klondike-Yukon Trail of '98. Although White Pass Summit, the trail's highest point was only 2,900 feet above sea level, winter temperatures reached 68 degrees below zero; summer ones soared to 95 degrees above zero. During the winter of 1897-98, 70 feet of snow fell, not in flakes but in small grains like sand, that compacted in drifts as hard as rock.

Even before the snow began to melt in 1898, a cable tramway was being constructed across the tundra and boulder fields that formed an almost impassable six miles of the trail between the summit at White Pass & Yukon Milepost 20 and Log Cabin at WP&Y Milepost 33. After its completion, Sourdoughs, the name given to the Klondikers because they existed on sourdough flapjacks and beans, could have their goods trammed across this part of the trail for a fee.

The immensity of the strike indicated a need for a permanent form of transportation. Thus, during the time the cable tramway was being built, men, materials and equipment had been steadily moving into Skagway to build a narrow gauge railroad from Skagway, Alaska to Whitehorse, Yukon Territory. Whitehorse was the staging point 111 miles from Skagway where most Klondike-bound gold rushers paused to recuperate and organize for the long trip ahead to Dawson City. The first six miles of the White Pass and Yukon Railroad were put in service on July 21, 1898 and were used to haul construction supplies to the beginning of the climb to the summit at a tent town named Dyea. The WP&Y named this location Rocky Point, and it is here that the railroad first meets and crosses the Trail of '98, the original route of the Klondike gold rusherees. From this point on, the WP&Y almost entirely follows this early trail.

DEAD HORSE GULCH

Dead Horse Gulch is 20 miles from Skagway. It is here that an estimated 3,000 horses were killed in falls from the steep mountainside into the gulch. To bypass this obstacle, the railroad built a high, long, spidery steel arch trestle over Dyea Creek. When I visited the area in June, 1976, less than a third of this trestle was left protruding over the gulch. I estimated that its original length was nearly 2,000 feet, and it had been suspended at least 750 feet over the bottom of Dead Horse Gulch. It must have been awesome when it was in use, and I can hardly conceive of men hardy and brave (or foolhardy) enough to have worked on it during construction or later to have taken trains across it.

This bridge must have made the Union Pacific trestle at Dale Creek, Wyoming, the Colorado Midland trestle near Buena Vista, Colorado and even the automobile suspension bridge at Royal Gorge, Colorado look like kid stuff. In March, 1973 while my wife and I were on a tour of Western Mexico, we rode the Chihuahua al Pacifico from las Mochis to the summit at Creel, Mexico and went by four-wheel drive into the Barranca del Cobra (Copper Canyon), the Grand Canyon of Mexico, to stay several days on a Mexican rancho. On the return trip, I got into a discussion with a well-traveled railfan. He told me that if I thought the Chihuahua al Pacific or the narrow gauge lines of the Rio Grande epitomized the building or operation of a railroad under extreme conditions, I should ride the WP&Y. When I finally saw this line in June, 1976, I realized the

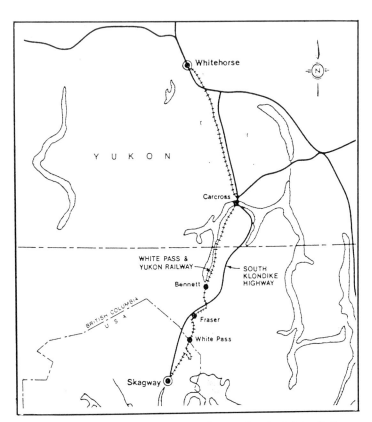

The WP&Y ran for 84 years from the height of the Klondike Gold Rush to its end when world metal prices plummeted and the mines at Yukon shut down. This privately owned railroad reopened in May, 1988 and is one of the last narrow gauges in North America today. The WP&Y has one of the steepest grades. From sea level at Skagway it climbs to 2,885 feet to White Pass.

man was right. All other railroads were child's play compared to the building of the first 40.6 miles of the WP&Y from sea level at Skagway, Alaska to an elevation of approximately 2,500 feet at Bennett, B.C. The remaining 70 miles to Whitehorse was at relatively waterline level.

By late 1900, the WP&Y had built a railroad into Whitehorse and was busy hauling miners and their impedimenta into the Yukon Territory and then back to Skagway after they had made their strike and were enroute to the States. There was little or no freight to haul back to Skagway.

WWII SPARKS CONSTRUCTION

In June, 1942 the Japanese occupied Attu, the westernmost Aleutian Island located off the coast of the Alaska Peninsula, and construction of defense works had to be expedited in Alaska. Vulnerable sea lanes mandated land supplies; by November, 1942 the 1,428-mile Alaskan-Canadian Military Highway (ALCAN) bound Alaska to Canadian railheads. This route, however, could not take care of all the demands, and the rehabilitation and augmentation of the WP&Y was begun immediately. Because it was a narrow gauge railroad, seven of the Rio Grande's K-28 (470s), as well as a number of passenger and freight cars and some work equipment, were quickly conscripted.

The steel trestle over Dyea Creek was approaching obsolescence at this time, so a line change was mandatory. The mountain walls were blasted away, or in several cases, cribs were anchored to the walls as appropriate. A 1,000-ft. long tunnel near the summit was bored through an obstructing point and much gravel ballast was hauled from available moraines to counter the effects of permafrost. The rehabilitation project took advantage of the summer's 20 hours of daylight, and the flow of soldiers, other personnel and supplies was soon continuous.

The rehabilitation and the line change were of such quality that the condition of the road was above average when I rode it in 1976; however, it was apparent that the WP&Y was heading towards the same fate as the Rio Grande narrow gauge. The only freight being handled was a tri-weekly train of fuel oil moving to points along the line, particularly to Whitehorse, and even here trucks operating on the ALCAN threatened to pirate this trade.

The WP&Y suffered from declining passenger business operations, just as the Rio Grande had, and it soon reverted to freight only. Finally, in 1982, that too stopped. Later, in 1988, abbreviated railfan excursion runs were started. These trains traveled from Skagway to Fraser, 28 miles northeast of Skagway and three miles north of the summit, and back. The experience is something like the Durango to Silverton excursion, but the scenery is more magnificent and the route is much more historic.

Pulling into Leadville, Colorado. *Colorado State Historical Society*

Two Union Pacific, Denver & Gulf men wait at Como, Colorado in 1900. *Colorado State Historical Society*

Denver, South Park and Pacific locomotives. *Colorado State Historical Society*

Carbonate Hill serviced by the Denver, South Park & Pacific at Leadville, Colorado. *Colorado State Historical Society*

Another view of Leadville, Colorado provides a view of Mount Massive in the background. *Colorado State Historical Society*

A typical day at the Colorado Midland depot and station at Leadville, Colorado. *Colorado State Historical Society*

DSP&P's Como Roundhouse

Here is another relic and reminder of the time when the Rocky Mountain Empire was dependent on iron rails and iron-hard men to transport the materials needed to build the empire and to carry its resources to market. This is the remains of the Denver South Park & Pacific roundhouse at Como, Colorado, once an active division point and terminal on the DSP&P line between Denver and Nathrop, Colorado.

Today, the Como community has been somewhat restored, although it is now dependent on railfans and other tourists. During the 1970s it was a hippy community. When these young people matured and became responsible adults, they rebuilt much of old Como. Now, they maintain a better than average restaurant and other amenities. You can still ramble among some of the old DSP&P relics, though, and listen to the ghosts talk.

These are the remains of the DSP&P roundhouse as they appeared in 1942 at Como, Colorado, once an active division point and terminal on the line between Denver and Nathrop. *M.D. McCarter collection*

An exquisite DSP&P Mason Bogie locomotive. *Colorado State Historical Society*

A Rio Grande "main line" caboose waits in Colorado. *Don Heimburger collection*

D&RGW Engine No. 1552, a 4-8-2, at Helper, Utah, October 1, 1947. *R.H. Kindig*

44

OVE AND BELOW: Newly constructed and freshly painted D&RGW cars display "the action road" logo.
n Heimburger collection

Baldwin's Unique Mallets

Uintah Railway Engine #51 was one of two unique locomotives built by Baldwin based on a design proposed by Lucien C. Sprague, general manager of the Uintah. They were high pressure, articulated engines with a 2-6-6-2 wheel arrangement and 42,000 pounds of tractive force. Water was carried in a pair of tanks located on either side of the boiler, and bituminous coal was used as fuel. Eighty-two percent of the engine's weight rested above the twelve drivers. Actually, the concept should have produced greater tractive force than it did. By comparison, Rio Grande's 480s (K-36, 2-8-2s) had 36,200 pounds of tractive force and the 490s (K-37) had 37,100 pounds.

These engines were commonly called mallets. In fact, only the mechanical people, who always insisted on being accurate in their classifications, did not refer to them as mallets, regardless of their appearance, which clearly showed that they had four-cylinder simple engines. The pilot, which was articulated to better negotiate the heavy curves found on the Uintah, contributed to their resemblance to mallets.

The first of these engines to be delivered, #50, had crown sheets angled to compensate for six percent grades, and it was necessary to be especially cautious at a grade called Moro Castle to be sure that water covered the sheet at all times. Engine #51, when delivered, had been modified to eliminate this fault.

ABOVE: Hauling a train of sacked gilsonite, Uintah Railway Engine No. 51, pauses for a drink at one of the water tanks along its line.
BELOW: A right side view of brand new Engine No. 51. *Colorado State Historical Society*

U.S. Battle Utes Over Gilsonite

In the northeast corner of Utah there is a Ute Indian reservation, or at least the vestigial remains of one. In 1863 the United States government signed a treaty with the Indians which stated that all land east of the Continental Divide belonged to the Americans, and all the land to the west belonged to the Indians. It was a clearly defined division with one exception: The Indians ceded all mineral rights on their portion for $10,000 in cash.

In 1868, the Americans decided they had given the Indians too much land. Thus, outright land ownership was changed to the concept of reservations. This culminated in the 1878 Meeker Massacre. The Utes were still recalcitrant; holdouts were moved by the U.S. Army to a reservation near Vernal, Utah.

Shortly thereafter, a wandering prospector discovered an unidentified black substance in the seams of the sedimentary rock in one section of the reservation. There was a lot of it, and as it turned out it did not exist anyplace else in the world.

Samuel Henry Gilson experimented with it and found that it was a rare black hydrocarbon that could be used to make superb paints, varnishes, lacquers and an insulating material that was impervious to corrosion from any chemicals. Later, high test gasoline and metallurgic coke would be derived from it.

GILSONITE MINE OPENS

In partnership with a man named Seaboldt,

Gilson opened a mine of the substance, which was now named gilsonite. The mine was on the Ute reservation and the Army and Indian agent ran the Utes off.

History had repeated itself. With an immense deposit of valuable material in sight, the Americans were not about to let the Indians garner the shekels. By an Act of Congress in May, 1888, a triangular piece of land measuring 7,000 acres was withdrawn from the reservation. A survey had shown that all the gilsonite was confined within this acreage. The U.S. had agreed to pay the Utes $20 per acre for the land, but there was one knotty stipulation in the Congressional legislation: all adult Utes had to agree to and sign the treaty validating the Act.

WHISKEY LURE

This posed a real problem: how to get the Utes to assemble at a specific location on a given date. Gilson and Seaboldt met with the Indian agent, territorial authorities and Army personnel to devise a way to effect a meeting. None of the ideas seemed feasible, but then Seaboldt came up with what he considered to be a sure way. He believed that the promise of all the whiskey they could drink without being hassled would bring every Ute to the meeting.

The Army instantly demurred on the basis that it was unlawful to sell whiskey to Indians. Seaboldt replied that there would be no sales. He planned to supply the liquour and give it to the Indians. Thus, it was agreed. The date and the location were set, and arrangements were made to estab-

Uintah Railway Engine No. 50, the first of two to be delivered, was designed to accommodate steep six percent grades. *Colorado State Historical Society*

lish a tent city for the meeting. Then messengers were dispatched to each tribal unit to disseminate the information. Each clan or tribal chief was informed sub rosa that there would be all the free whiskey the Indians could drink, and that they would not be restricted by the agency or the military while doing so.

The tent city was set up. Seaboldt brought in several wagonloads of whiskey. The Utes came early and set up their camp near the meeting place. On a warm, sunny day in September, 1888, the treaty was laid out in one of the open-ended tents. The Indians lined up, and soldiers unloaded whiskey kegs from the wagon and broached them with blows of their rifle stocks. As each adult signed or made his or her thumb print, he was told to go get his liquor. By nightfall, all those eligible had done so and wandered away to sleep off the free drinks. The next morning a few latecomers, who may even have been repeat signers, appeared. The Army wanted to be sure that all the necessary signatures or thumb prints had been obtained, so the treaty was brought out again and another keg was broached.

The Whiskey Tent Treaty became effective, and the area was opened for exploitation. It quickly spawned a settlement known as the Duschesne Strip that, for depravity, lawlessness, murder and licentiousness, rivaled any of the infamous Union Pacific "Hells on Wheels" or wild cow towns.

UINTAH RAILWAY

It soon became apparent that a railroad would be needed if the gilsonite deposits were to reach full profitability. Thus, the Uintah Railway was incorporated in 1903. By early 1905, 53 miles were in operation from Mack, Colorado on the Denver & Rio Grande to Dragon, Utah. The road was capitalized by Bert Carlton and Spencer Pentrose, two men who had become rich from gold mines at Cripple Creek.

The line left Mack by the north, veered west and entered Utah at Milepost 50 via Baxter Pass, elevation 8,431 feet. An earlier dirt road ran from Mack to Dinosaur, Colorado. This was not a satisfactory road, and after the Rangely oil field was opened, Highway #139 was built via Douglas Pass, elevation 8,268 feet. This highway is paved and at Douglas Pass runs about 10 miles due east of Baxter Pass. The old road, which closely followed the Uintah rail line, can be negotiated in good weather, although a four-wheel drive is recommended. There are few relics of the old line left to see, which was abandoned in 1938, and less of the station and community remains.

Watson, Utah, 62 miles from Mack, was the northern terminal. Including short branches to mines, the Uintah totaled 72 miles. Other than Dragon and Watson, the list of stations included Atchee, just out of Mack where the railroad shops were located, Wendella, Sewell and Rainbow Junction.

Uintah freight cars, mostly flatcars and one passenger combine, were built at Atchee. The other two Uintah passenger cars were obtained from the Rio Grande Western. They had been used on the RGW when it was narrow gauge. The Uintah ran one roundtrip passenger train daily. Ordinarily the consist was an engine and one car.

The UR owned five Shay engines, a Baldwin Consolidation and two saddleback engines. It bought one Mikado, Engine #11, built by Baldwin. On delivery, the Mikado was found to have too long a wheelbase to negotiate the curves south of Baxter Pass. With much effort, the drivers were swung free and the engine was towed to Watson for use north of Baxter Pass. When an inventory of Shay replacement parts was taken, enough were found on hand, with the exception of a boiler, to build another Shay engine. A boiler was obtained from the Lima Company and Engine #2 was put together at Atchee.

IMPLAUSIBLE CURVES

Grades and curvatures on the UR were almost incredible. It took 50 minutes to ascend the six miles from Atchee to Baxter Pass and 40 minutes to descend the seven miles from Baxter Pass to

A Uintah Railway daily passenger train crew poses with Engine No. 10 and one combination car. *Colorado State Historical Society*

This Uintah Railway train rounds the bend on the east side of Baxter Pass. This is probably a special — a daily train usually had only one combination car. Note that the long passenger cars were alternated with short freight cars in the consist in order to negotiate sharp curves. *Colorado State Historical Society*

Here the daily rounds Baxter Pass on the west side. Both the engine and combination car badly need paint jobs as the lettering has completely worn off. *Colorado State Historical Society*

Wendella. Lucius Beebe, in *Narrow Gauge in the Rockies*, gives the governing grade on the Uintah as 7.5 percent. Almost all of the short branches and some segments of the main line did have this grade. This explains the heavy reliance on Shay engines. Beebe also states, however, that there were curves of 66 degrees. This is either a misprint or Beebe is exaggerating when one considers that a right angle is 90 degrees and that a 66-degree curve is only 24 degrees from being a right angle. This is hardly possible even if the apocryphal story that all Uintah equipment had no corners were true—the basis for this story being that sharper turns could be made without the corners touching. There were several 24-degree curves on the Silverton Branch of the Rio Grande narrow gauge and one of nearly 27 degrees in Monero Canyon, west of Chama, New Mexico, that was realigned to 24 degrees. This was considered to be the maximum that was feasible. The same was true on the Rio Grande Southern.

Gilsonite was highly volatile. Sparks from engines occasionally set fire to the burlap bagged material loaded on flatbed cars. Derailments, some more accurately called wrecks, occurred. The Uintah was not a cynosure, certainly not

what you'd expect a railroad to be. More highways were built and trucks were improved so that much of the production began being hauled to Craig, Colorado to be transported over the Rio Grande. Authority for abandonment came in 1938. In 1957, Barber Oil, a subsidiary of Standard Oil of California, installed a 18-mile long slurry pipeline and pumped the gilsonite slurry from Bonanza to a new plant built at the Rio Grande station at Gilsonite, Colorado, between Fruita and Mack.

The story of the Uintah is a touching one. A wandering prospector discovered an unknown substance not found anywhere else in the world. The Army and Bureau of Indian Affairs closed its eyes to an entire Indian tribe being euchered out of potential wealth, legally theirs, by being given copious amounts of whiskey. An incredible, seemingly impossible railroad was built and operated to have the wealth gained by infamy. Progress caught up with it, and it was abandoned.

The wasteland quickly began to claim its own, and now it is only with difficulty that any signs of railroad can be found. In the Duschesne Strip, except for gutted crevices in the sedimentary rock, even fewer mementos remain.

Chapter 4
Denver & Rio Grande Standard Gauge

Late in the 1950s, information began seeping out to the railroad industry that Krauss-Maffei in Germany was developing a new concept of locomotive powering that could possibly be better than a diesel-electric. The revolutionary concept was a transmission of power to the 40-inch diameter wheels by a geared-hydraulic drive. Prototypes of these 4,000 hp locomotives, eventually built in 1961, were well received and successful in German railroad operations.

As efficient as they were, the diesel-electrics did have some faults. American railroads were interested in the Krauss engines, which had 104,100 pounds of tractive effort. Representatives, including some from the Southern Pacific and the Denver & Rio Grande Western, went to Germany to observe the locomotive and possibly buy a few. By early fall 1961, there were three of these engines on the Rio Grande and the same number on the SP. They were accompanied by teams of German technicians.

KMs ON THE SP

By 1962 the Krauss-Maffeis were in actual train service on the SP. The SP used the engines at or near sea level and apparently was satisfied with their performance. This was not true on the Rio Grande, and in a chance meeting on the sidewalks of San Francisco, G.B. Aydelott, then president of the Rio Grande, sold the Rio Grande KM units #4001, #4002 and #4003 to the president of the SP.

These engines are listed in the Rio Grande equipment rosters of 1962 and 1963 only. They went to the SP during 1963. Their departure from the Rio Grande occurred with a great deal less fanfare than their arrival.

PROBLEMS ON THE D&RGW

The Krauss-Maffei engines were observed and tested by the D&RGW and the SP representatives under German railroad operating conditions. These conditions, to some extent, matched those on the SP which explains why they had less headaches with the German-built hydraulics than the Rio Grande. The problems these locomotives caused for the Rio Grande were insurmountable, and their departure to the SP saw no mourners. Factors which contributed to their failure on the D&RGW included high altitudes, heavy grades, extreme swings in the climate and differing modes of engine use.

In Germany the engines operated at or near sea level. Baltic height, or German mountain heights, range from 300 to 1,000 feet. In the Harz Mountains the highest point, Brocken Peak, is only 3,747 feet. In Bavaria, the Alps tower up to 10,000 feet, but this is not German railroad country as most of the industries are in the plains country. German climate is temperate and uniform. The country is about 500 miles north to south and 250 to 500 miles east to west.

DIFFERING TOPOGRAPHY

Whether hauling a train east-west or north-south, an engine could leave one German border early in the morning and reach the other border shortly after dark. At the arrival terminal, it had all night to be inspected and serviced for the following day's work. The Germans also filtered their fuel oil.

Now consider the differences on the Rio Grande. Denver has an elevation of 5,280 feet, the Moffat Tunnel apex is 9,239 feet, Tennessee Pass is 10,221 feet and Soldier Summit's peak is 7,440 feet. The lowest point on the Rio Grande main line is Green River, Utah at 4,066 feet. Salt Lake City's lowest point is 4,233 feet and Pueblo's is 4,672 feet.

The amount of oxygen in the atmosphere at 1,000 feet, or even at 3,747 on Brocken Peak is much greater than at 5,000 to 10,000 feet. The Krauss-Maffeis did not deliver their rated horsepower and tended to "flame out" or die at the higher elevations such as the Moffat Tunnel.

Krauss-Maffei D&RGW Engine No. 4001 is pictured in a profile of the engineman's side. *Orvil Benson*

Temperatures at Green River in the summer can range from 80 to 110 degrees in the middle of the day. Winter temperature can range from a mild 60 to 70 degrees to lows of minus 30 to minus 40. Summers may be hot and dry with occasional heavy rainfall while winters may be very cold with heavy snowfall. All of these factors were detrimental to the Krauss-Maffeis' construction and performance.

Germany's entire square mileage is slightly less than that of Montana. Its greatest width at any point is 500 miles. In contrast, it is 745 miles from Denver to Salt Lake City and 626 miles from Salt Lake City to Pueblo. Diesel-electric power was expected to handle a train virtually nonstop between the eastern and western terminals and, after as little as three hours for servic-

ing, turn around and make the run in the opposite direction, receive another short servicing and then make the trip yet again. The diesel-electrics were seldom shut down but instead were left idling between runs. This kind of service could not be achieved by the Krauss-Maffeis.

TOO MANY FAIL-SAFES

The truck/power drive assembly of the Krauss-Maffei was weak as well. The SP had to remodel these with the assistance of EMD. Also, because they were of German design, these engines had many fail-safes. Another consideration in their performances was the fuel oil. In Germany it was filtered; here it was plant-run.

All in all, the Krauss-Maffeis were a beautiful German dream that, on the Rio Grande, turned into a Rocky Mountain nightmare.

Here is a head-on view of Krauss-Maffei D&RGW Engine No. 4001. The apparent dirt on the right side of the locomotive is only a trick of lighting; there was not a blemish on the engine's finish when this photo was taken. *Orvil Benson*

This is the rear end view of Krauss-Maffei D&RGW Engine No. 4001. *Orvil Benson*

This is an end-to-end top view of the Krauss-Maffei truck/hydraulic drive assembly. TOP RIGHT: An interior view of the control cab of K-M D&RGW Engine No. 4001 taken at the K-M works in Germany. Note that German railcars with German stenciling can be seen through the engineman's window. BOTTOM RIGHT: This is a side view of the truck and transmission of power of the K-M engine. This design was one of the frailties of the diesel-hydraulic concept. *Orvil Benson*

Krauss-Maffei D&RGW Engines No. 4001, 4002 and 4003 coupled to a dynamometer car and hauling a westbound train west of Rifle, Colorado in early November of 1961. *Orvil Benson*

This is the same train as the one on the previous page hauling freight between Westwater and Cisco, Utah. *Orvil Benson*

Here are the three K-M engines (Nos. 4001, 4002, and 4003) coupled with a dynamometer car being serviced at Grand Junction, Colorado in November of 1961. They provide a combination of 12,000 hp, 990,870 lbs. of weight on the drivers and 312,300 lbs. of tractive effort. *Orvil Benson*

The cause of this freak accident on the Colorado Midland at Rifle, Colorado remains a mystery. Engine No. 31 at the left has been involved in some way because its tender is missing and there is collision damage at the rear of the cab. The other engine, which is loaded on and halfway through stock car No. 4261, is missing its tender too. There is also a damaged and burned-out engine boiler at the right, apparently on its trucks. As usual at a railroad wreck, a lot of thrill seekers have shown up to get in the way. *Denver Public Library*

Chapter 5

Colorado Midland
Standard Gauge

Threat to the D&RG

The Colorado Midland was chartered in 1883 as a standard gauge railroad to run from Colorado Springs to Leadville-Aspen. Almost immediately, this new line threatened to be a competitor to the Denver & Rio Grande for the traffic from this mining district.

Construction did not start until April, 1886, but the road was completed to Buena Vista, Colorado in 1887. In Colorado, the route went through Florissant, Hartsell and Lake George. At Trout Creek Pass, the divide between South Park and the Arkansas drainage, the CM passed the Denver, South Park & Pacific by means of an overpass. Leadville was reached in 1888 and building continued on towards Aspen. The Continental Divide between the Arkansas and the Roaring

Fork rivers was pierced at an elevation of 11,258 feet by the Hagerman Tunnel, which was 2,061 feet long. Railroad operation over this pass was almost impossible in the winter.

NEW TUNNEL BORED

To better the conditions, the Busk-Ivanhoe Tunnel was bored 580 feet lower than the Hagerman. The latter tunnel eliminated 13 snowsheds and 12 bridges and tunnels. The 1.78-mile long Busk-Ivanhoe Tunnel was a great improvement over the Hagerman. After the CM rails were pulled in 1921, the tunnel was renamed the Carlton Tunnel and converted to use as an automobile route. At that time it was not wide enough for two-lane traffic, so automobiles had to move alternately east-west and then west-east.

To counter the threat of the CM in Aspen, the D&RG built frantically from Redcliff, Colorado to

Glenwood and then up the Roaring Fork, arriving in Aspen on November 7, 1887. The CM built to Basalt and then on to Aspen, where it arrived before the end of the year. It was the first standard gauge railroad to cross the Rocky Mountains of Colorado. The D&RG had already gleaned all the glory by arriving first.

The CM then decided to try a standard gauge line to Utah, and it continued building down the Roaring Fork River to Glenwood Springs. From there it went westward on the south side of the Colorado (Grand) River. It reached Newcastle, Colorado in 1889.

RAILROADS COMBINE

To avoid a costly race between Newcastle and Grand Junction, the D&RG and the CM negotiated a contract by which the two railroads transferred their interests between Rifle, Colorado and Grand Junction to a jointly-owned third organization: The Rio Grande Junction Railroad.

The CM was sold to the Atchison, Topeka & Santa Fe in 1890. It went into the hands of a receiver in 1894, ceased operations in 1918 and was dismantled in 1921. For some inexplicable reason, the United States Railroad Administration of World War I did not look kindly upon the CM and did not favor it with any of the railroad funds being spent so freely elsewhere.

In 1967 a route for Interstate 70 was chosen that involved several miles of Rio Grande trackage near Glenwood Springs. The line change was plotted on the south side of the river now called the Colorado, and it used 7.5 miles of the old abandoned CM grade.

FATAL FIRE

The two railroads successfully operated the Rio Grande Junction Railroad with only a few mishaps or misunderstandings. In September, 1897, however, there was one tragic collision between a D&RG passenger train and CM freight train near Newcastle. At least 25 lives were lost, possibly more, because of an unquenchable fire which broke out after the collision.

The Interstate 70 line change was the finest thing that could have happened for the Rio Grande management. It eliminated the long steel bridge over the Colorado River at Glenwood Springs that was a steady nightmare for Rio Grande executives. They were constantly worrying about it collapsing or being the scene of a wreck that would effectively close the railroad for a protracted period of time.

This Colorado Midland passenger train — composed of Engine No. 25, a combination car and three coaches — was photographed at the Colorado Midland station at Glenwood Springs, Colorado. Look at all the derby hats, vests, swallow-tailed coats and gold watch chains. The fireboy must have worked all night wiping and polishing that engine to make it so bright. Back in the days when each engineer was assigned an engine, the fireboy did not go to sleep until the "injine" was spick-and-span. Note the single-pump air compressor and the ties which have been hacked to lineal length, instead of being sawed, and are hewed. There are no fishplates, and the crossing shows only buggy and wagon wheel tracks crossing it. *Denver Public Library*

A summertime excursion train consisting of a doubleheader, six coaches and a baggage car paused here at Devil's Slide on the Colorado Midland. *Colorado State Historical Society*

This is Hellgate — also known as Hagerman's Pass — on the Colorado Midland. *W.H. Jackson/Colorado State Historical Society*

Colorado Midland Engine No. 17 pulls a baggage and mail car and a passenger car across the high, spindly steel trestle overlooking the Upper Arkansas River area near Buena Vista, Colorado. *W.H. Jackson/Colorado State Historical Society*

This shot was taken on the Colorado Midland along the Frying Pan River approaching Basalt, Colorado. *W.H. Jackson/Colorado State Historical Society*

Chapter 6
Major Standard Gauge Railroads

During the merger mania among railroads in the late 60s and early 70s, I was assigned to evaluate the GM&O, which the Rio Grande considered in its plans for a route from Denver to Chicago. I was impressed by the highly maintained and orderly conditions of its entire plant. In my opinion there was no other railroad, including the Rio Grande, that could equal its standards.

All tracks, including the auxiliary ones, were in perfect alignment, ballast was clean, and ties were ballast level with none broken or out of line. Ditches were clean, and the communication lines had each pole protected by fire-retardant, cleared areas. *Don Heimburger collection*

Gulf, Mobile & Ohio

During the period of the late 1960s to mid-70s when all railroads were feverish to merge, sell or abandon, the Rio Grande was right in the fray. It contested a number of these transactions, tried to be included in others and explored possible acquisitions of others.

I was assigned the chore during those years to make inspections, evaluations and reports in connection with many lines under consideration and to be the line's expert witness in operating matters before the ICC and state utility commissions. In those years, I covered and studied an estimated 40,000 miles of railroads. After retirement, as an independent consultant working for groups and communities fighting abandonments of railroads considered vital to their interests, I traveled over another estimated 10,000 miles of railroads.

GM&O-IC MERGER

The one railroad I took the greatest pleasure in working was the Gulf, Mobile & Ohio at the time the Illinois Central was trying to merge with it. The Denver & Rio Grande Western got involved and hoped to acquire the GM&O for a Kansas City to St. Louis and Chicago route in case we got in on the Union Pacific-Chicago Rock Island & Pacific merger. It was later ruled we could not do so.

One of the most unusual and memorable structures I saw on these many miles of railroad was the station at Roodhouse, Illinois on the GM&O. It was built on land at the point where the St. Louis line diverged from the Chicago line. Using money the GM&O was determined the IC would not get, it had upgraded its property until it was as pretty as a new, little red wagon. It was a beautiful example of what a railroad should be.

Although the GM&O operated more rail miles and served a territory of greater extent than the Rio Grande, the two roads had many similar features and much in common. They were both profitable, well managed, innovative and maintained in excellent condition. Both managements were

Illinois Central Engine No. 2817, a 2-10-2, pulls a long train of 121 cars of freight at Eddyville, Kentucky on December 22, 1957. *Harold Stirton*

GM&O Engine No. 280 is a six-axle model diesel-electric. This model was produced and bought early in the change over period from steam to diesel and sold to railroads that had a special need for a bit more tractive effort than the four-axle models. They were more popular on lines that enjoyed a favorable grade approaching the optimum of .009 percent with maximum curvature somewhere in the range between three degrees and six degrees.

The theory behind the six-axle model was that the power plant in the carbody of the unit could produce power to feed to the six motors (on the axles) as well as it could to four.

After complete dieselization became a fact, manufacturers began producing more efficient and less costly four-axle units that gave an additional advantage of multiple unit combinations. With the demise of passenger trains that eliminated the need for higher speeds over long distances, railroads came to use freight type units almost exclusively. The method of adjusting power by adding or reducing units in each combination became prevalent. *Don Heimburger collection*

ABOVE: True to the GM&O's reputation for operating immaculate locomotives over well maintained tracks, GM&O Engine No. 255 rolls through a late fall countryside. It is reminiscent of scenes along the tracks between Roodhouse and Springfield, Illinois. Some idea of the date may be found in the lettering on the footboards, "Be Careful." Shortly before the end of steam and the beginning of all diesel operation most railroads, concerned about footboard related injuries, stenciled them like this. Finally they just issued mandatory instructions that footboards would not be used. In many cases the footboards were simply removed from engines. *Don Heimburger collection*

This IC Engine No. 2800, a 2-10-2, with 57 cars of hot freight, pulls through at Dyersville, Iowa in August of 1947. The photographer must have bribed the fireman to get such a spectacular plume of smoke. *Harold Stirton*

BELOW: IC Engine No. 2605, another 2-10-2, with a clean fire, is just two cars short of 100. Why, oh why, couldn't the IC-GMO merger activity have been back in the days of steam so I could have reveled in scenes such as this while I was gathering material for testimony at the ICC hearing? In a month spent along the IC, all I ever saw were diesels. *Harold Stirton*

GM&O Engine No. 880-B poses a question. This is the lead and control unit. When this type diesel-electric engine was put into service, and for a considerable period thereafter, each multiple unit combination (usually four units) was designated by a number for the lead control unit plus the letter "A". The trailing non-controlled units between the "A" units were called "B" units and so numbered.

The ICC prescribed that, for accounting purposes, each unit have an individual identity. This ridiculous rule for a very short time required train orders to carry the numbers of all units in the combination in rotation from the lead unit. You better believe that the screams issuing from train dispatcher offices across the land quickly caused this rule to be rescinded.

The pockmarks on the nose of the engine were not uncommon. They could be caused by hailstones, by gravel or coal falling from cars on adjacent tracks, by hunters with shotguns wanting something to shoot, and in pheasant country, especially across Kansas and Nebraska, by the engines hitting pheasants in flight. In the latter case the impact made a single dent.

The stylized GM&O blazon replaced the predecessor's emblem of the lettering GM&N in a circle. *Don Heimburger collection*

The GM&O acquired, among other things from its predecessor the GM&N, the habit of maintaining clean, shiny engines and immaculate work areas.

GM&N Engine No. 425, a 4-6-2, on a turntable. Hopefully, the employee governing the turning will be sure to line it up properly. On the Rio Grande we had a few instances where this was not the case, and engines, including a unit of a diesel locomotive, went into the turntable pit. Two of the steam engines were C-48's, a whole lot smaller than Engine No. 425.

Apparently the GM&N expected their road crews to handle their own minor derailments, for a heavy chain and rerailing frog were carried along the bottom of the tender. *Don Heimburger collection*

competent, and the operating people were capable and loyal to their employers. Both roads were more than ordinarily service oriented.

Both dated from about the same period following the end of the war between the states or the early 1870s. The Rio Grande opened the Rocky Mountain Empire; the predecessor system later called the GM&O provided a transportation system almost totally destroyed during the recent conflict between the states. The D&RG's competition was a worthy opponent, the Union Pacific, while the GM&N faced the emerging Rock Island system. The influence on the about to be born D&RG started about 1872. In 1870 the CRI&P gobbled up many of the small railroads either then operating or in the making in the South. The GM&N also wanted to establish suzerainty over this territory.

The competition between the UP and the D&RGW lasts to this day, while by 1900 most of the territorial struggle between the GM&N and the RI had just about entered a standoff stage. The Rock Island eventually became a target for acquisition by merger with the Union Pacific. The GM&O, because of its excellent condition, profitability and surplus cash, became the target for the Illinois Central.

During the UP-Rock Island debacle, the condition of the Rock Island became deplorable and after even the UP lost interest, went bankrupt and ceased operations. The GM&O unsuccessfully fought takeover, and the resulting system became the Illinois Central Gulf Railroad Company.

MAJOR GM&N ROUTES

Essentially the GM&N, by the first decade of this century, comprised a system from the Gulf of Mexico northward through Mississippi, Tennessee and St. Louis to Chicago.

From the Gulf to Jackson, Tennessee, the GM&N had three lines: the western line originated at New Orleans and ran north to Jackson, Mississippi then eastward to Meridian, Mississippi via Union. At Union, it crossed the middle route of the GM&N.

Two south to north routes began at Mobile. One, the middle route ran via Union, Mississippi to Jackson, Tennessee.

At Jackson to St. Louis via Cairo there was only one main line, but there was an important branch from Jackson to Hickman, Kentucky. This branch intersected the IC at Dyersburg, Tennessee.

From St. Louis to Chicago, the main line ran via Springfield and Bloomington, Illinois. An east-

GM&O Engine No. 500 pulls into a yard towing a train of tank cars and two box cars.

The flat cars at right center with latticed bulkheads were used to haul pulpwood or turpentine pine loads cut to lengths the width of the car body and loaded crosswise of the body. The cars are of an old vintage and never used in interstate movements now.

The structure at lower right appears to be an inspection pit. In early years ICC rules required a rolling inspection of the underside of cars by carmen at some locations where certain prescribed operating conditions existed. *Don Heimburger collection*

As conservative as the GM&N management was, and usually devoid of the urge to keep up with or outdo its competitors, it did succumb to an industry-wide tendency to go it alone to build individual passenger depots.

This one is a prime example of such foolishness. There were numerous other examples to be found on American and Canadian railroads. This is also true in other countries around the world where moving by passenger train was the prime means of transportation. The building of these monstrosities was not always governed by a wish to outdo the Joneses.

The GM&N's passenger station at New Orleans brings to mind a situation I am more familiar with on the Rio Grande at Salt Lake City. There the D&RGW and Union Pacific wasted fortunes on building, operating and maintaining separate stations less than a mile apart, simply each to outdo the other. *Don Heimburger collection*

IC Engine No. 2805 has a train of 78 cars at Center Grove, Iowa on May 30, 1949. The IC ran many scheduled freight trains, as this is one of the few photographs of a freight train on this line flying white flags designating it was an "extra." *Harold Stirton*

west line ran from Springfield to Kansas City via Roodhouse, Illinois. At Roodhouse, a line branched off and ran south to St. Louis. This was the portion of the GM&O the D&RGW made an effort to acquire as part of the eventual final settlement of the UP-RI merger attempt.

The GM&O from the Gulf to St. Louis operated through an area where much of the western portion of the War Between the States was fought. As finally assembled, in addition to its main construction, it consisted of many small local railroads that were built to serve the South in the aftermath of the war.

RAILROADS SERVICE RIVER PORTS

At the beginning of the war there were only about 6,000 miles of railroad in the South. Cotton was king and almost all was produced along waterways that were navigable. Most of these rivers flowed north to south and eventually to the Gulf, providing ideal transportation by river boats. Any railroads were basically short east to west lines built to provide a specific means of transportation locally to a river port.

A small railroad was built in Louisiana just north of Lake Pontchartrain in the year 1831. It was probably the first railroad dismantled by the Confederates as they retreated from New Orleans. All rail, other track material (OTM) and rolling stock was moved during the retreat and used to rebuild a railroad in an area secure from the Yankees. As the war progressed, this plan of moving track material and rolling stock from threatened areas to secure areas was often resorted to by the Confederates. The Union forces did the same on a lesser scale.

CONFEDERATES DESTROY CORINTH

The pattern of retreat closely followed the eventual route of the GM&O up through Bogalusa in the far northeastern corner of Louisiana to arrive at Corinth in Mississippi's northeast corner. Corinth was developed into one of the major railroad hubs of the Confederacy. Union forces drove against Corinth so strongly it became apparent the Confederates could not save it. They started a retreat. To prevent the valuable railroad rolling stock and rail from falling into Union hands to be used against the South, on May 29, 1862 Corinth, with its crucial wealth of supplies and railroad necessaries, was completely destroyed by the Confederates.

A QUALITY RAILROAD EMERGES

The smoke and disruption of the War Between the States had hardly begun to settle before the GM&N began its building of a proud, service-oriented rail system that extended from the Gulf to the Great Lakes. Its ultimate accolade is that is did so without the hoopla, fanfare and scandals that attended the building of many other contemporary

This passenger station on the GM&O is one of the most unusual and memorable structures that I have seen on the thousands of miles of railroads I have traversed in my life. The GM&O tracks on the left run to Chicago; on the right they stretch to St. Louis. *John Norwood*

systems. Its history is a far cry from the many accusations of wrongdoing the Union Pacific-Central Pacific brought out.

I spent the greater part of a summer evaluating the GM&O, most of the time north of St. Louis and west to Kansas City. I was overwhelmed by the high state of maintenance; the well designed and constructed bridges which were present in profusion; the cleanliness of the station grounds; the excellent condition of engines and cars; and the sense of family and belonging displayed by all employees.

When it was ruled that the Rio Grande could not be part of endeavors to prevent the IC taking over the GM&O because the Rio Grande had no physical rail connection with the GM&O, and for the same reason was prevented from acquiring it, I was loaned to the Kansas City Southern. The KCS could enter the fray in opposition, and I was assigned to assist their attorneys and contribute information I had accumulated.

The merger did go through and a fine integrated rail system was flushed down the drain. Recognition by railfans and historians that it was a super rail system that contributed to the rebuilding of a nation torn asunder by a bloody, senseless war, can soften the loss. And, the knowledge that at least one word, "Gulf", remained in the new name, Illinois Central Gulf.

Train time at Bogalusa, Louisiana, a peaceful town in the deep South. It was only a hamlet, or less, at the time the rebel forces retreating from New Orleans went through the area carrying the salvaged materials to build another railroad when the escape from Union forces was assured. The town has grown to a respectable population of nearly 20,000.

This picture was taken at a time when GM&N was still operating steam. Note the coaling facility that fueled locomotives from either the main line or a spur. And, the GM&N was still in the less-than-carload freight business. A box car is unloading at the detached freighthouse across from the coal chute.

During the transition period to diesel, many railroads attempted to control the expense of providing passenger service by using motor cars, commonly nicknamed doodlebugs, that usually had the motor in the point and a mail-baggage-express section at the rear. This one is trailing two coaches, but in many cases where the passenger load was small, the doodlebugs also contained a passenger section.

Both the station and freighthouse are of rather old construction and heated by stoves rather than furnaces.

The blazon bears the letters of the predecessor, GM&N. This train was proudly named the *Rebel*.

Doodlebugs had many profiles or configurations and their origin was claimed by many. On the Rio Grande there was that infamous version built by Budd. The narrow gauge had them also on the Rio Grande Southern, called the *Galloping Geese*. Otto Mears built one for use on the Silverton Northern; and McClintock used a homemade one on the San Luis Valley Southern. *Don Heimburger collection*

Passengers enjoy a close-up view of the scenic beauty on this GM&O trip. *Don Heimburger collection*

ABOVE: GM&O Engine No. 407 gets its bunker filled the hard way using a skip filled by coal dumped through a grizzly from a car spotted on a low ramp.

The skip, after being loaded, is elevated to the unloading position up an incline of two rails upon which the skip wheels move. The force to raise the skip is provided by a counterbalanced cable running over a block and pulled down by a steam- or air-driven piston-cylinder arrangement mounted in the truncated A-frame to the right of the engine.

Note the roofless pickle vat-type water tank. Also note that this must be at a period before footboards were stenciled "Be Careful" and at a location where refueling was not done frequently enough to require a more efficient method. *Don Heimburger collection*

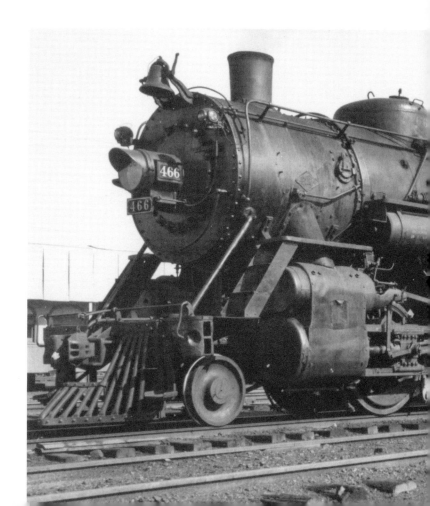

ABOVE: GM&O Engine No. 1515, an Alco, spanking brand new at the American Locomotive Co. plant at Schenectady. This is one of an order of four for the GM&O. It is a new 1,600 hp road switcher, often called "geeps" by railroaders because they were often denoted by the designation "GP" standing for "General Purpose."

The GM&O was one of the first major American railroads to be completely dieselized. *Don Heimburger collection*

GM&O Engine No. 466, a 2-8-2, all shined up with a full bunker of coal awaiting a call. The EPA would have no complaint about the emission from its smokestack. Some engine watchman is doing an expert job keeping her hot but showing only a trace of a plume. *Don Heimburger collection*

Railroads, telegraph, telephone and electric power systems early on placed demands upon the lumber industry for forest products, demands that required selected timbers and specialized milling. On the railroads, no entirely satisfactory substitute for wooden crossties has been developed. For communication and power transmission, tall, straight, element-resistant poles are needed. This busy interlocking plant clearly pictures the importance of lumber, seldom given its just due. *Don Heimburger collection*

Atchison, Topeka & Santa Fe Engine No. 3405, a 4-6-2, with the second section *Grand Canyon Limited* approaches 21st Street Crossing, Chicago. *Harold Stirton*

Atchison, Topeka & Santa Fe

The destination of the Santa Fe Trail was Santa Fe, New Mexico, and the goal of the traders plying this trail was the trade of the most active town in the Southwest. Even before the wagons quit rolling, men were dreaming of a railroad to serve the town and reap the profits of its trade.

There were two men preeminently involved: General William Jackson Palmer of the Denver & Rio Grande Railroad and Colonel Cyrus K. Holliday of the Atchison, Topeka & Santa Fe. Eventually, the AT&SF arrived first, but by that time Santa Fe was no longer the shining goal it had been earlier.

The AT&SF was chartered in Kansas in 1859 as the Atchison & Topeka Railroad, but national financial conditions and the Civil War soon intervened. Construction finally began at Topeka in 1869. On April 26, 1869 Holliday ran an excursion train to the end of the track, seven miles from Topeka. Later, at a gala picnic arranged for his guests, he made a bombastic speech. He predicted that Topeka, with a population of 700 people, would be the

eastern end of a rail system that would reach to San Francisco and the Pacific, to the Gulf of Mexico and to Mexico and to that greatly desired goal, Santa Fe.

The Pacific Railroad Act of 1862 established the authority for the government to give land grants to encourage and help pay for railroads building westward. Holliday was given a huge grant under these conditions, but it stipulated that he must reach the boundary of Colorado Territory by March 3, 1873. Colorado was still a territory at this date and did not become a state until August, 1876.

HOLLIDAY'S PREDICTIONS EMERGE

To validate Holliday's statements that he was going to build a road to the West, the railroad's name was changed. It became the Atchison, Topeka & Santa Fe. In the years that followed, most of Holliday's grandiose promises made in 1869 were brought to fruition. The Santa Fe became a 12,000-mile colossus.

This is AT&SF Engine No. 2919, a 4-8-4, pulling an eastbound freight through Kansas City in 1949.

Between 1965 and 1970 I spent a lot of time in the Argentine yard of the AT&SF, but by then it was all diesels. I well remember in 1927-28 sitting on a rocky point on Raton Pass and thrilling to the roar of Santa Fe jacks on the roll and roaring arrogantly as they cut the grade of Raton Pass down to size.

AT&SF engines always seemed to roar, unlike the Grande locomotives that just seemed to chug along as they hauled coal out of Trinidad where my father was the telegrapher.

It was hard for me to understand why he worked for a dinky road like the D&RGW when he could work for a real railroad. He always said, "I've worked for a lot of lines, but if I live to be 100, never let it be said I worked a day for that scabby outfit." Dad lived to be 101 years old. *Phil Korst*

Atchison, Topeka & Santa Fe Engine No. 2654, photographed here at Santa Fe, New Mexico on June 27, 1969 is a far cry from the steamers that came in from Lamy Junction and the Denver & Rio Grande Western narrow gauge C-Class of the early days of this bustling town. *M.D. McCarter collection*

This photo was taken in the winter of 1947. Atchison, Topeka & Santa Fe Engine No. 3754, a 4-8-4 Class 3751, is southbound at Colorado Springs passing the Rio Grande-Rock Island depot on the D&RGW segment of the paired trackage between Denver and Pueblo, Colorado. *M.D. McCarter collection*

Colorado Territory was reached by the deadline and capital became easier to acquire. The road continued towards the Pacific via Albuquerque, New Mexico. As surveys were made ahead of the construction, it became apparent that it was not feasible to build directly into Santa Fe. Also, by that time, Santa Fe was no longer so attractive.

To appease the irate people of Santa Fe and, indirectly, all other New Mexicans, the AT&SF promised to build a branch off the main line from Lamy Junction, 18 miles from the New Mexico capitol. The branch was completed in February, 1880, although no wye had yet been provided. The first train arrived in Santa Fe after backing up the entire distance. It was powered by two engines: the *A.G. Greeley*, a Baldwin 4-6-0, and the *Marion*, a Tauton 4-6-0. Governor Lew Wallace, who also authored *Ben Hur*, drove the last spike.

The people of Santa Fe, however, were oriented northward toward the San Luis Valley in Colorado and the original Mexican colonies strung along the Rio Grande del Norte. They were not satisfied with the AT&SF Lamy Branch. Two months before the arrival of the AT&SF, the Texas, Santa Fe and Northern Railroad, a narrow gauge line, was chartered.

TERRITORY DISPUTES STALL PROGRESS

The people of Santa Fe were not only disgruntled by the AT&SF actions, they had been given a bitter pill in February, 1880 when the D&RG was restrained from building further south under the

Atchison, Topeka & Santa Fe Engine No. 1460 was a 4-4-2 Class 1452. Note the unusual placement of the illuminated engine identification board on the front end. *M.D. McCarter collection*

provisions of the Treaty of Boston or the Tripartite Agreement. This was a negotiated agreement designed to settle disputes between the D&RG and the AT&SF which stemmed from claims of territory invasions by each party. The D&RG, at the time, had graded to a point called White Rock, several miles beyond the soon-to-be-established town of

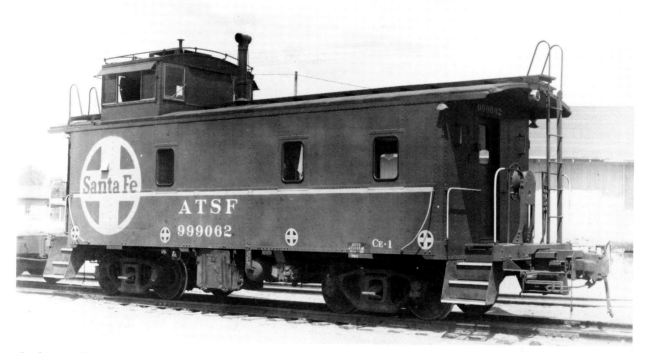

Atchison, Topeka & Santa Fe caboose No. 999062 is seen resting at Santa Fe, New Mexico in May, 1969. At the time of this picture, the D&RGW had been gone from Santa Fe for more than 25 years. This town was once considered a goal for rail's end for the AT&SF; it ultimately became just a spur end from Lamy Junction, the AT&SF main line. *M.D. McCarter collection*

Espanola, New Mexico. The laying of rail, however, stopped before it reached White Rock. An area surrounding the confluence of the Chama River and the Rio Grande River was deemed the best place for an end-of-rail town to be built while the D&RG waited out the ten year life of the Tripartite Agreement.

The town of Espanola thus sprung into being, 34 miles from Santa Fe. New Mexicans then incorporated the TS&N on December 9, 1880. The AT&SF charged that this was only a subterfuge of Palmer to continue building toward Santa Fe, and many others thought the same, possibly with some justification.

This dispute and other factors involving finances, right-of-way difficulties, and the tendency of the New Mexicans of that time to quarrel among themselves, delayed construction. The TS&N finally reached Espanola on February 8, 1887 and began interchanging business with the D&RG. The AT&SF unilaterally broke the Treaty of Boston, and the D&RG was able to legally acquire and operate the TS&N in 1890. Unfortunately, Palmer was not around when his earlier dream of building to Santa Fe was achieved. Of course, neither was the Golden Fleece sought by both Palmer and Holliday, the active business town of Santa Fe.

Today, the AT&SF still operates the Lamy Branch, but the D&RGW Santa Fe branch was last operated in 1941, and rail was picked up from Santa Fe to Antonito, Colorado in 1942.

Union Pacific

Historically, the Union Pacific, the Atchison, Topeka & Santa Fe and the Denver & Rio Grande Western have been extremely fierce competitors and, at times, bitter enemies. Time and changing conditions have resolved most of the issues, however. Any remaining antipathy is on a corporate level or between the traffic departments.

In towns where people are employed by two or more of these railroads, employees do not hold it against each other that they work for different roads. Personally, I have hunted, fished, fraternized and drunk with many who worked for the UP or the Santa Fe. I have even broken bread and eaten salt with them. There have been no ill effects. The food was just as savory and the booze and beer were just as satisfying.

John C. Kenefick, later to be president of the UP, came to Alamosa, Colorado as superintendent when I was trainmaster. This was late 1951 or early 1952. Kenefick was from the UP, but at the same time he was persona non grata there. G.B. Aydelott, president of the Rio Grande hired him. When things had cooled off, Kenefick returned to the UP and started his climb all over.

Union Pacific Engine No. 9503, pictured on April 12, 1952 at North Platte, Nebraska was a 4-12-2, an oil-burner and a big hunk of iron that could pull many tons across Nebraska and Wyoming. The "X" in front of the engine number shows that the train is running as an extra. *M.D. McCarter collection*

As assistant chief transportation officer on the Rio Grande, in 1962, my specific duty was making operating studies. At that time, we were looking closely at whether we should move our Grand Junction, Colorado humpyard, close it or improve it. North Platte, Nebraska — on the UP — had one of the most efficient and modern hump operations in the country. By this time Kenefick was again in favor and in authority on the UP.

I wrote him requesting permission to observe their operation at North Platte. His reply came back promptly, a true bit of Kenefickism, "Sure, come on over as my guest and see what a real railroad is like."

Kenefick was too busy to spend much time with me, but I was introduced around and told to go where I wanted, when I wanted and ask any question desired. My first visit to the yard was at night, and I felt like the rube from the country on his first visit to New York City. It was difficult to keep my perspective and not feel like the poor relation.

A *REAL* HUMPYARD

North Platte was actually two humpyards. There was an east hump and a west hump. An eastbound train did not have to wait for classification while a westbound one was being worked. There were even separate fueling and servicing tracks. Mobile vehicles and radios expedited the operations about the yard by personnel. The illumination of the yard was the icing on the cake. Towers and lights on high cables strung across the yard make it unnecessary for switchmen or mud-hops to carry lanterns. At any point, from entrance to exit switch, you could easily read a newspaper at night. The light bills must have been enormous, but so were the operating advantages.

Union Pacific Engine No. 4019, a 4-8-8-4, is "balling the jack" with a mile of freight cars behind it near Cheyenne, Wyoming in the summer of 1954. *M.D. McCarter collection*

I stayed for a week, and after the first day of watching a real railroad in operation I diligently observed and made notes. Of course, the Rio Grande did not have the millions of dollars available from resources other than the railroad, but there were many points that could be used to improve our own yard operations. When asked if I would like to have an escorted tour of the entire line I jumped at the chance.

W.B. (Pete) Groome, head of the UP safety department, took me to the west end at Ogden. He was a very knowledgeable and capable escort. We had some common ground because Groome's brother-in-law, W.J. Gill, was the Rio Grande roadmaster at Denver. On our return east, Pete spent a day with me at Cheyenne. This was especially welcomed by me for the UP had only recently centralized their train dispatching, and we were in the planning stage of doing the same.

All that I saw confirmed my belief that money could do just about anything. One fact I had stored away: If the Rio Grande had all the up-to-date equipment and ready cash, under proper circumstances, we could take a train east or west between Denver or Pueblo and Salt Lake City about three hours faster than the UP could.

This was during the time when traffic departments were riding the horse named Speed to death. Patrons had yet to awaken to the truth that speed, or actual traveling time, was not the governing factor of service. Eventually, they realized this and recognized that what counted was the time involved from loading to delivery at destination on schedule.

SHORT-FAST TRAINS

With the blessings of our traffic department, the Rio Grande came up with a first in the railroad industry and inaugurated its SFT trains. Competitive schedules were reduced coast to coast accordingly. Patrons had not wised up yet, and for two or three years we took enough transcontinental business from the UP and the AT&SF to really hurt them. Most of the damage was done to the UP because it served the Central Transcontinental Corridor with us; the AT&SF and the Southern Pacific-Chicago, Rock Island & Pacific routes were far enough south that they were not affected much.

This operating concept had other benefits: It was both economic and efficient. Facilities and operation of helper engine points at Tabernash, Colorado and Thistle, Utah were eliminated. We quit helping westbound trains over Tennessee Pass, although we had to continue to help the eastbound trains from Minturn, Colorado. Only coal trains were helped westbound out of Helper, Utah. With the faster turning of power and less time on the road, utilization of engines and cars increased greatly. A proposed order for additional engines became unnecessary and was cancelled. Train and engine service employees liked the system because under the Hours-of-Service Act, which was 16 hours at that time, they could double the road more often in a 24-hour period.

RUN THROUGH CONCEPT

Neither the UP nor the Santa Fe were asleep at the switch very long, however. Using the efficiency of the North Platte yard on the UP and Argentine

After railroads began using each other's power indiscriminately, the situation turned into a power distributor's nightmare. In this shot, taken in the fall of 1969 at Kelso, Washington, Denver & Rio Grande Western Engine No. 5336, a geep with 3,600 hp, is coupled between Union Pacific Engines No. 3647 and No. 3645. *M.D. McCarter collection*

UP Engine No. 5304, a 2-10-2 oilburner, is at Green River, Wyoming in 1957. Prior to dieselization, the UP loaned or leased this class of engine to the Utah Railway. *M.D. McCarter collection*

The UP and D&RG never got together to build one Union Station in Salt Lake City. Here, UP Engine No. 948, an E-9 diesel-electric, is arriving at the UP Salt Lake City station. *M.D. McCarter collection*

yard on the Santa Fe, they developed the concept of "run through" trains. These were switched, classified and made up in a superyard to run through all intermediate terminals without the delay attendant upon multiple switching enroute. Anyway, it was fun making our traditional competitors squirm for a while.

It is a new ball game today. Patrons woke up to the fallacy of speed, and railroad management picked up the cue and learned that cooperative and non-competitive operations were the way to go.

UP Engines No. 1277 and No. 766 pull a passenger train over the Spider Web Bridge at Dale Creek. This bridge was not used after 1901 because rolling stock had become too heavy. It took men with iron nerves to highball across bridges like this. *W.H. Jackson/Colorado State Historical Society*

Three early diesel units dedicated to the *City of San Francisco* sit highlighted by patches of melting drifted snow in Green River, Wyoming. *Union Pacific Railroad photo*

Union Pacific *City of San Francisco* is powered by a three-unit diesel combination. The lead and rear units are stenciled SF-1; the middle unit SF-5. I am not certain of what method the UP used but apparently they were so prosperous they could buy enough power to allow them to dedicate units to given trains.

The emblems of the three partners in this named train combination — UP, C&NW and SP — all appear on the lead unit. However, the UP has demonstrated its suzerainty by placing a large distinctive UP emblem above the others. *Union Pacific Railroad*

Union Pacific *City of Denver* leaves town enroute east. The smokestack of the old smelter in Globeville has not yet been demolished, and in the background are the Rocky Mountain foothills There are still patches of snow on them.

Surprising is the fact that on the nose where the emblems of the participating railroads are displayed, the Chicago & North Western emblem is above that of the Union Pacific. This is analogous to displaying a state flag above Old Glory. *Union Pacific Railroad photo*

The UP succumbed to a current fad and destroyed the appeal and brute beauty of an otherwise legendary steam engine by covering it with a "tin can" disguise.

This 4-8-4 Pacific type is at the head end of the "49er". In the illuminated engine number box at the left top front of the engine, it appears that instead of an engine number there is a "49" — the train designation.

Just below left center past the engine's nose is the radiator and hood of a 1927 model "tin lizzie". *Union Pacific Railroad photo, Glen A. Kratt*

ABOVE: American's first streamliner, built in 1934, is seen here with Engine No. M-10000. The cars consisted of one unit marked United States Mail Railway Post Office and two coaches.

This combination was named the *City of Salina*; the train was scrapped in 1943. *Don Heimburger collection*

Union Pacific *Los Angeles Limited* was exclusively a Union Pacific train. The units are not as polished as those on the *City of San Francisco* and neither are the cars. This does not mean it was not an excellent train and well regarded by the public.

Power is a three-unit combination, two A and one B unit. The lead unit is numbered 50-M-2, and the B unit is 50-M-1.

Interestingly this picture was shot at the same location on the Union Pacific, Riview, as the one of the *City of San Francisco*. *Union Pacific Railroad*

This photograph captures a Kansas City Southern 4-6-2 hauling a four-car passenger train across ballasted deck Bridge No. A-675 near Leesville, Louisiana. *M.D. McCarter collection*

The Kansas City Southern had a number of locomotives such as Engine No. 1002. *M.D. McCarter collection*

Kansas City Southern-Frisco

That boomer operator, my father, developed a yen for the Ozarks and the South in general after just a couple of years in the West. Thus, we packed up the trunks and suitcases and went off to relocate once again.

First we went to the White River division of the Missouri Pacific, then to the St. Louis-San Francisco (Frisco) and finally to the Kansas City Southern where my father was on that road's seniority list for the second time. We lived for short periods in various small town in Arkansas, Kansas and Missouri. By the early 1920s the Organization of Railroad Telegraphers had successfully converted the railroads to the philosophy that telegraphers and station agents who had given up jumping from railroad to railroad deserved consideration. Job vacancies were bulletined, and the bidder with the most seniority was awarded the job. Boomers took what was left over or worked the "extra board."

Back on the KCS, for some reason, Dad was successful bidder for the agency at Westville, Oklahoma. Westville was an active and prosperous community of about 1,000 people. Located in the northeast corner of Oklahoma a few miles from the Arkansas line, it was the crossing point of the KCS and a branch of the Frisco that stemmed from its main line near Fort Smith, Arkansas. Following the 1923 railroad strike, the freight and passenger service on both of these roads was good.

Westville was heavily populated by Cherokee Indians. In fact, possibly half of the population was Cherokee. They were industrious farmers and livestock raisers: a fine race of people.

CHICKEN SALE DAY

In the fall, numerous carloads of fat hogs and cattle were loaded at the stockyard north of town. Every so often, the owner of the local produce house lined up the farmers for a chicken-shipping day. On that day, farmers and their wives showed up early with homemade crates full of chickens. The noise of squawking chickens and roosters challenging each other was deafening. So, too, was the noise of some of the domestic disputes around the produce house. Traditionally, the butter, egg and chicken money belonged to the wives, yet, and again traditionally, bargains were sealed and money was paid to the husbands. Often, there was hell to pay when some husband did not willingly hand over the chicken money to his frau. The poultry was shipped live in specially designed poultry cars.

Westville was almost modern. It even had a waterworks, of sorts. The water was piped around town, but each home was permitted only one outlet in the kitchen. Consequently, no one had water closets, not even the bank president. Residents of Westville were ahead of their time in recognizing the danger of water pollution through the soil, however. Each home had an outdoor two-holer: an outhouse with a big hole in the seat for

My father worked briefly as a telegrapher around 1921 or 1922 at Pittsburgh, Kansas where this photo of Kansas City Southern Engine No. 1008 was taken on March 17, 1937. *M. D. McCarter collection*

the adults and a smaller one for the children. Instead of being built over a pit, there was a container below the throne. This box had a hinged door at the back so the town scavenger could clean it out twice a month. There were two boxes inside the privy: one held old newspapers and catalogs for the women to use and the other was full of soft corncobs for the men. We quickly learned there was a right way and a wrong way to turn the cob when using it.

I was part of a coterie of four boys: two whites and two Cherokees. In summer, as quickly as our chores were done, we gathered and left the town's environs. Before we took off, we pooled our finances to buy a plug of Brown Mule chewing tobacco, which cost five cents at that time, and sometimes to restock our supply of fishhooks and sinkers.

EARLY RAILFANS

Our favorite fishing hole was on Shell Branch, a small, slow-flowing stream with a few frothy holes at driftwood jams. There were hundreds of sunfish, usually blue gills, and once in awhile we caught a catfish which weighed a couple of pounds. The best part of this location was its proximity to the KCS tracks. Every time a train whistled north or south we hurriedly set our poles and rushed to a stone wall near the track. There we sat, counted cars, smelled the coal smoke and gloried in the sight and sound of the locomotives. I

think we all dreamed that maybe someday we would be there on the right side of such an engine, pulling the whistle cord and yelling at the fire boy, "Come on, boy. Get that fire hot. We're running late!"

Some days, when we did not want to fish, we went down to the waterworks near the KCS-Frisco crossing and sat in the shade to watch trains, just like today's railfans. The KCS was senior at the crossing, and the Frisco trains had to stop and send a flagman to the crossing. At the crossing, this flagman had to open a box on the telegraph pole and contact my father to get authority to proceed. Arkansas once posted a rule for railroads at crossings that read, "Two trains approaching a railroad crossing at grade will each stop, and neither will proceed until the other has gone." Of course it was soon amended, but it did get into print.

We spent a lot of time speculating about what would happen if, someday when a KSC train was passing, the Frisco train could not stop. We loved to sit in the shade and dream of being an engineer or eating on one of the passing diners. I guess that part of the attraction to young boys that we were, was thinking that just maybe, a Frisco train might someday run into a KCS train, and we would be there to witness it.

I used to see engines such as this St. Louis-San Francisco (Frisco) Engine No. 1400, photographed August 25, 1936 at Ft. Smith, Arkansas in 1923-25 when I lived in Westville, Oklahoma where the Frisco crossed the Kansas City Southern tracks. *M.D. McCarter collection*

Rock Island

My matriculation and initial introduction to the world of expert witnesses came about when I was assigned as one of a team of four to make an acquisition study of the Colorado & Southern-Fort Worth and Denver-Burlington-Rock Island line from Wendover, Wyoming to Galveston, Texas. At this time, the Burlington Northern was seriously considering selling this line to the Rio Grande. Such a sale would have given the Rio Grande a north-south transcontinental route free of major competition from the northwest Pacific Coast areas to the Gulf of Mexico. It was a very desirable possibility. Unfortunately, the BN became aware of the same potentiality before the sale was consummated.

Before the deal was called off, however, I had earned the equivalent of a B.A. degree in railroad studies. The curriculum included acquisition, evaluation, rehabilitation-maintenance and traffic potential. Some of my dearest friends insinuated that instead of earning a B.A. degree I was, in fact, earning a B.S. degree referring, of course, to the excreta of a male bovine.

At least, when I was assigned to work the Union Pacific-Chicago, Rock Island & Pacific merger case, I was not going into terra incognita. During the several years that this case dragged on, I earned my Ph.D degree.

WITNESS QUALIFICATIONS

An expert witness must first of all have an impressive title for status. To get this I was promoted to Assistant Vice President of Operations.

He must also have demonstrated experience in his background. This did not present a problem.

He must also be a bit of an actor, a mountebank. This comes along with your mother's milk if you are born Irish. Ad-libbing is considered crucial, too. The part that requires more study and application is the ability to confuse and disconcert the persons who are doing the interrogating. Obfuscation is a valuable art, but it must never be done in a manner that will antagonize the Interstate Commerce Commission or the state utility commissioners. It must be confined to opposition lawyers and their expert witnesses. It goes without saying that an expert witness always remains calm and patient and keeps his temper. Properly done, it is easy to make interrogators blow their stacks. Finally, you never, ever trust a lawyer, no matter how many meals or drinks he buys you. This is tantamount to saying that you must learn at just what point you dump the free beverages on the floor under the table.

Underlying all this must be the true fact that the expert witness really is an expert. The integrity of the witness statements and testimony must be verifiable and accurate.

RIO GRANDE PROTESTS

Just as the acquisition case was breaking down, the ICC announced a second hearing on the BN merger case. The Rio Grande and others for some reason had not filed as protestants in the first round. They were smarter this time, and they soon filed their complaints. R.L. (Bob) Jacobsen and I

CRI&P caboose No. 17073 at Tucumari, New Mexico, June 20, 1976. This was a place of interest to the D&RGW during the UP-Rock Island merger case in the late 60s. *M.D. McCarter collection*

Trackside view of Southern Pacific's Tucumcari station on September 18, 1978. *M.D. McCarter collection*

Tower at ATSF-GM&O crossing at Joliet, Illinois on October 21, 1967. Union Station is just beyond. *M.D. McCarter collection*

Rock Island Engine No. 655 pulls the *Quad Cities Rocket* at Blue Island on November 1, 1970. I rode this once while engaged in the UP-RI merger case. It was not in the *California Zephyr* class but was a fine train. *M.D. McCarter collection*

Rock Island No. 1 *Jet Rocket* at speed on July 24, 1957 is one of the extravaganzas that helped bring down the once proud Ri. It was a concept a quarter century ahead of its time. *M.D. McCarter collection*

CRI&P caboose No. 17132, a steel bay window style at Council Bluffs, Iowa on December 26, 1972. This design was very popular with trainmen. *M.D. McCarter collection*

were told to get going and develop all the adverse things we could.

Our first stop was the BN offices in the Twin Cities. There, we got maps and information of the location of vital points and crew change terminals but not much more; the BN was not exactly friendly. However, on the eve of St. Patrick's Day with a temperature of at least minus 30 degrees, we did find a warm tavern and joined many Swedes, Finns and one or two sons of Erin celebrating the removal of all the snakes from that green isle across the Atlantic.

We had just a little time then, in Denver, to get clean clothes and visit our treasury for a new supply of money and to buy tickets to Seattle. Unfortunately, with all that expense money in our purses, the morning after our arrival was diamond clear so we had to work. We took pictures of the BN yards and facilities from a helicopter and then saddled up and started east for a month of hedge-hopping or working during the day and flying at night. On the ground or from helicopters, we put together a comprehensive picture comparing what the BN claimed it needed versus what had been or was being done.

AERIAL VIEW

At Duluth no helicopter was available. We had to settle for a four-seat airplane. With the door on my side removed, we flew over the docks and facilities at Superior, Wisconsin and found that, contrary to BN claims, high-cost repairs were not needed. Iron ore was not being transhipped. Two years earlier, the process and methods changed when taconite replaced crude iron ore.

The Rio Grande and other protestants did not win that round, but the BN merger was held up for a year. Then the UP-CRI&P merger exploded. Again, there was no alternative. The Rio Grande had to protest.

The Denver & Rio Grande Western had relations with the CRI&P, commonly called the Rock Island, since 1888 when the CRI&P came to Colorado Springs and negotiated a trackage agreement to Pueblo and Denver. That same year the Rock Island entered Denver with a trackage agreement with the UP from Limon, Colorado to Denver and an agreement with the Denver & Rio Grande for terminal use.

Other than this relationship, we did not know much about the Rock Island. We had to find out fast, and it had to be in detail.

SCARY ROUNDTRIP

The *Denver Rocket* was still running at this time, so the fastest way to get a quick look was a roundtrip on it to Chicago. Because we were accustomed to the heavy metallic slag that the Rio Grande used for ballast, that ride was frightening for us. The Rock Island used a chat ballast brought up from the area around Ft. Sill, Oklahoma. It was eas-

ily placed and worked. It drained well and apparently satisfied Rock Island people. We were dumbfounded, however, as we stood at the vestibule door on the last car of the *Rocket*. Behind the train, the rails were a series of lessening snake tracks. Under the moving wheels they moved sideways to form "s" shapes. Then the tension of the rails brought them back into alignment in the loose, noncohesive ballast.

In our investigations and studies, we found the Rock Island people from section men, to corporate heads, very cooperative. Eventually, the UP put the pressure on and we had to go underground, however, there was never a time that the people who worked on the Rock Island line itself did not support our efforts. Facts and figures were made available to us that were not even available to Rock Island or UP corporate heads.

The Rio Grande was mostly interested in a Denver-Council Bluffs and a Denver-Kansas City- St. Louis route. In the following years, I spent much time, with or without the knowledge of the Rock Island, between Limon, Colorado, Belleville, Kansas and Omaha, Nebraska. The situation of the Tucumcari-Southern Pacific connection had to be explored, as well as its effect on the Belleville-Manhattan-Kansas City segment. I also studied branch lines, including the Horton Branch. It was in fair shape from Fairbury, Nebraska to Beatrice, Nebraska. From Horton, Kansas, once the major mechanical repair point on the Rock Island, to Topeka, Kansas, it was almost inoperable.

LAVISH HEADQUARTERS

I'll never forget my first visit to the Rock Island offices on LaSalle Street in Chicago. From that visit I had no idea of whether or not the UP would get the Rock Island, but I became convinced that the Rock Island was well on the way to bankruptcy. Even in the offices of the billion dollar corporations of today, there is nothing to equal or approach it. On the executive floor the walls were covered with real monk's cloth and original oil paintings and watercolors by well-known artists. The plants were in expensive pots, and there were fresh flowers on each desk. All the while, soft music played.

The fairest flower of all sat at the reception desk, and this face changed every 30 days. Originally, this was a stunning beauty with auburn hair falling in small waves to below her shoulders. Her voice, as she greeted me, was pure southern treacle. Starlets were hired by the Rock Island for 30-day tenures as receptionists, and each month they became more luscious. Until I became sort of persona non grata on the Rock Island, I made an honest effort to visit the Rock Island offices on LaSalle Street soon after I figured there had been a change of starlets. Of course, they were there

ABOVE: About one year later on April 11, 1971 the same engine powering the same train taken at Bensenville, about 20 miles from Chicago, begins to show the effects of Milwaukee's financial condition. *William Raia collection*

ABOVE RIGHT: Milwaukee Engine No. 30-C hauls a "city" train at Franklin Park, Illinois and shows a good paint job and maintenance. On May 17, 1970 these trains were still enjoying a fair passenger load as evidenced by the number of cars in the train. By the time I was here in 1972, the train load had materially decreased. *William Raia collection*

This Milwaukee Engine No. 34A pulls a long string of varnish passing Pacific Junction in Chicago; it likewise shows the suffering maintenance as paint peels on the engine's prow. *William Raia collection*

CRI&P Engine No. 628 EMD leaves Peoria, Illinois on May 30, 1966 with a passenger train and one TOFC load. RI tried several innovations in an effort to stave off disaster, but it didn't help. *M.D. McCarter collection*

for atmosphere only and were not accessible, but — Oh Lord! — they were viewable.

At long last, the hearings before the ICC began. The first rounds were held in Chicago. I spent the weeks in the hearing room accompanied by Rio Grande lawyers. We had quarters at the Union League Club. For the most part, the representatives of other railroads, except the UP, stayed there also. Before this stage had finished I had become very cynical and dubious about lawyers.

At lunch I was welcomed by groups of lawyers, and I listened to them decide who would be crucified that afternoon. At dinner, sometimes attended by the afternoon's victim, the group would reach a consensus about who would get the shaft the next day.

HEARINGS CONCLUDE

The hearings eventually moved to Denver and then concluded in San Francisco. I was present at each day's session for the entire process, except for about a week in San Francisco.

Our lawyers deemed it best that I be incommunicado until it was time for my appearance on the stand. If ever you are held as a house prisoner, by all means do it at the Clift House in San Francisco. That week was pure heaven.

During my testimony, I was able to get the Missouri Pacific attorney so confused and frustrated that he asked the same question, a long involved one, five times. The examiner finally told him that I had answered the question over and over again and that he, the examiner, had understood the answer, so "please move on to the next question." The attorney broke his pencil, threw it on the desk before him and said, "No more questions."

The hearing concluded, and it was time for a blowout. San Francisco allows topless waitresses, so we made reservations at one of the more risque bars. This promised to be a new experience for a boy from the boondocks. I went along willingly, even eagerly.

Because it was a blowout and the attorneys were picking up the tab, I ordered Irish on the rocks; Bushmill's no less. It was served in a large glass. I could just savor the first sip. As the waitress leaned over to place it before me, one of her rather large breasts flopped into the drink. This ol' boy decided he did not want his whiskey contaminated. I went back to the Clift House, sat at the bar under the polished redwood burls, ordered some more Bushmill's and charged it to our attorney.

The UP-CRI&P merger was the spectacle of the century, and I'm glad I was privileged to be involved in it.

In 1879 engineers drew up plans for what is now the Cumbres & Toltec Railroad, and the line entered Chama, New Mexico a year later, with additional construction continuing to Animas City near Durango. Here, a K-36 2-8-2 plys the iron in 1965, probably being used as a helper. *Chris Burritt*

Locomotive #487 leads a freight train over a short trestle on the Durango to Farmington line in 1965. In 1951 an unexpected boom came to this line when the Southern Union Gas Company notified the Rio Grande it wanted to ship 235 carloads of pipe to Farmington by rail. *Chris Burritt*

Called the *Green River*, this #340 1881 Baldwin-built C-19 2-8-0 with 18,947 pounds of tractive effort was renumbered to #400 in 1924. The stylish Consolidation sports a red-painted cab roof, sideboards on the tender and white-rimmed tires. *Photo by Clayton Tanner*

On the Cumbres line westbound in 1950, the miles click by as the narrow gauge train lumbers higher and higher over the valley floor; in the distance, forests of pine populate the mountain sides. The *San Juan*, train #215, ended its travels between Durango and Alamosa on February 1, 1951. *Clayton Tanner*

Built by Baldwin in 1896, #318 was called the *Goldfield* and was originally built for the Florence & Cripple Creek Railroad as their #8. It was sold to the D&RG in 1917 and renumbered #318. In 1954 it went to the Colorado Railroad Museum. *Clayton Tanner*

This is inside the Denver & Rio Grande Western's *Silver Vista* observation coach on August 12, 1950 as train #461 crosses a steel bridge on the Durango to Silverton line. Built in 1947 from car #0313, the *Silver Vista* was made in the railroad's own shops. The steel and glass roof afforded travelers a good view. *Clayton Tanner*

Just in from a laborious run upgrade to Silverton, the #473 K-36 Class 2-8-2, with 36,200 pounds of tractive effort and 195 pounds of boiler pressure, is rotated on the turntable at Durango in 1950. *Clayton Tanner*

Train time at Durango as the *San Juan* pulls into the station in the 1950s. Except for cosmetic changes, and some additions, the scene is the same today. Of course, the *San Juan* is now but a memory. *Clayton Tanner*

Except for a few locomotives, the Denver & Rio Grande remained faithful to Baldwin-built steamers on the Narrow Gauge, with the first big engines being class 125s (K-27s). The #493 was built in the road's own Burnham shops from Class 190 standard gauge locomotives. *Chris Burritt*

A weather-beaten 3000-series truss-rod box car with the flying "Rio Grande" lettering sits on a weed-grown siding in Farmington some 30 years ago. *Chris Burritt*

Engine No. 493 of the K-37 Class was rebuilt in 1928 from a standard gauge C-41; it was retired in 1970, stored at Alamosa. The K-37 locomotives were rebuilt at Burnham Shops. *Chris Burritt*

On a bright Colorado morning engine No. 492 gets coaled-up at the tipple in Chama prior to the next challenging run over Cumbres. The Rio Grande logo is visible over the window of the shed. *Chris Burritt*

In August of 1965 William A. Raia caught RI Engine No. 654 spick-and-span with a respectable *Golden State* train of varnish at Ottawa, Ilinois. Note the siding is weed grown; this condition of secondary tracks on the RI became more noticeable as the UP-RI merger case was prolonged. The equipment followed the same route. *William A. Raia collection*

This is CRI&P Engine No. 1915 on the Missouri-Arkansas line on May 9, 1959 sitting cold at Harrison, Arkansas, a once proud 2-8-0. *M.D. McCarter collection*

All decorated for a festive day in 1899 CRI&P Engine No. 894, a 4-6-0 sits in Goodland, Kansas. The engine still has an old cowcatcher, but an automatic coupler. *M.D. McCarter collection*

By August, 1968 when William A. Raia photographed Engine No. 632 pulling the *Cornhusker* at Joliet, Illinois, the polish was gone from engines and passenger cars. Note the sorry condition of the secondary track at the right — out of elevation, joints down and bad gauge — indicating lack of even primary maintenance. *William A. Raia collection*

Milwaukee Road streamlined diesel electric powered *Olympian Hiawatha* is shown in terrain reminiscent of scenes in the "Cascades of Washington," from the files of the Milwaukee Railroad public relations office. No railroad ever had such evenly spaced ties, or ballast so clean. Whether a touched-up photo, a photo of an artist's drawing or a montage, it deserves a place in railroad historical archives to be preserved for its verisimilitude. *Milwaukee Road*

Chapter 7
A Dilemma —
Too Many Photos

An Impossibility

A dedicated railfan would say he or she could never have too many photos. A fan will run all over the country, some even all over the world, and spend a fortune on photographic equipment and film in order to increase his or her photo collection.

Many are of such outstanding quality or depict a subject or a scene that the photographer railfan yearns to have it preserved and presented in a book for all of the fraternity to enjoy. The photo is sent to the author or publisher of fan-oriented books or magazines with hopes that it will be published.

And therein lies the dilemma. What is to be done if the book is to contain only 250 photos and a thousand must be sorted through to select the most appropriate ones? It is not unusual to run out of desk or table space in spreading these photos and resorting to the floor for greater area. By gradual elimination, a primary selection is made. Then a second, third and fourth sort is done before finding pictures you believe satisfactory. Even then there are instances of indecision, and it is not uncommon to go back through all the discarded photos to find one you have a recollection of that just might be more appropriate to the subject being written about.

During this process individual pictures that have no relation to the current book being composed are found and set aside because of their quality and because there is something in them that reminds you of a past experience.

HAUNTING IMAGES

All the time you are writing and typing the current book the presence of these pictures keep nagging at you and begging to be included. Each has incited a memory of having actually been there or the knowledge that it will revive a memory in some reader or demonstrate some facet of railroad history that should be preserved. It is

Milwaukee Engine No. 846 is on the point of a commuter train unloading at Elmwood Park, Illinois about seven miles east of Bensenville yard and two miles east of Franklin Park where the Milwaukee crossed the Soo. *Norm Schreiner collection*

ABOVE: Two Milwaukee yard goats are being serviced and ready for switching operations at Bensenville, Illinois. Engine No. 722 is just about ready to move. Engine No. 644 at the right has the blue flag in place to indicate workmen are still on or about the engine. *Norm Schreiner collection*

BELOW: Milwaukee boxcab electric Engine No. E8 at Deer Lodge, Montana in August of 1960. The first beef herd established in Montana was at Deer Lodge, and the area was visited by Isaac I. Stevens in 1853 while surveying a railroad route across South Dakota and Montana. *Don Heimburger collection*

unfortunate that these photos have only a modicum of information — just enough to make it possible to write a caption for them but not enough to spark a story.

This has been especially true in this book. Photos found during research, and photos sent to me or to the publisher have, in the course of selection, accumulated to the point that they simply cry out to be made available for viewing.

There were pictures of the New York Central, Great Northern, refrigerated cars replaced by mechanical refrigerators, Chicago, South Shore & South Bend Railroad, some locomotives of the Chicago, Burlington & Quincy, Soo Line, Wabash and even a Reading Camelback. Then there were pictures of the *Texas Eagle*, Chicago & North Western, Chicago Union Station, Pennsylvania boxcar X-29, a couple of gas-electric motor units, Northern Pacific and Minnesota & St. Paul mail and express cars, and an Illinois Terminal motor-coach combination.

It would be a discourtesy to the railfan fraternity not to publish them, yet none of them produced the spark to give the basis of a story, nor were they of a kind that I could connect with personal experiences of any specific nature of a remembered occurrence.

RAILROADING AND PERFUME

I kept mulling this over searching for a solution. Then one day the solution came in a form far removed from railroading.

My wedding anniversary was approaching and, in trying to think of something to get for my wife, I went into the Denver May D&F store to the cosmetic counter.

I told the salesgirl my problem, and she told me that all women loved perfumes that smelled nice and lingered. She brought out a tray of sample essences in spray bottles and asked for my hand. She sprayed samples at several spots on the front and back until there was one that for some reason brought a faint memory from the past. She had been quoting prices for quarter ounce flagons that went from $50 upward. The one I liked was $85. Now, my lady always smells good enough to me that I did not see that she needed an $85 quarter ounce of perfume to make her more alluring. I thanked the girl and said I thought I would look for something else.

Leaving the store and still inhaling the emanations from the samples sprayed on my hand, a recollection of a pleasant and pervading fragrance grew stronger. The recollection took me back almost years, yet was very clear and memorable. It

Chippewa Engine No. 3 steams into Chicago on November 25, 1937. *R.H. Kennedy*

further strengthened my conviction that ladies, singly or in a group, could smell nice without paying nearly $100 for a small bottle of perfume.

ARKANSAS CHURCH-WOMEN

I went back to a time in the hills of Arkansas when my mother took the whole family, except for my father who went fishing instead, to church on Sundays in a small, non-airconditioned, red brick building. Attendance was heavy and consisted to a large degree of nice ladies, quietly dressed and without makeup. Worshipers sat crammed in the pews, and they perspired. However, before the service was over that little church was smelling like a flower garden. It was a soothing, pleasurable and pervasive essence that made you think of roses, irises, sweet peas and other flowers.

Summer or winter, on Sundays that little church always had its noticeable and distinctive fragrance. When Ladies Aid or the Missionary Society met at our house for an afternoon our parlor had the same smell for a day or two.

I asked my mother about this one time, and she explained that during the summer as each flower was at its peak in the gardens the ladies went from garden to garden and gathered the sweetest smelling blossoms. The petals of these were dried, mixed with certain spices and stored in sealed jars to preserve their aroma. Small quantities of the potpourri were put in little sachets of loosely weave cloth.

A sachet was placed in each drawer containing items of the lady's clothing including her intimate apparel. A sachet was also pinned to or hung with each of her party or go-to-meeting dresses. The items of apparel absorbed the effusion from the potpourri to give the lady that subtle and appealing fragrance of all the flowers in a summer garden. I say subtle, but it must have been distinctive and strong, for 60 years later a whiff of outrageously priced perfume brought it back to me — and with the recollection, nostalgia.

The thought came to me: If those ladies could gather a collection of flower petals and put them to use in a manner that memories of the fragrance of summer flowers can be recalled and enjoyed years after the flower is gone, why can't I just put all those fine, memorable pictures in one inclusive chapter as a potpourri of pictures?

I hope it works, and that someone viewing one or more of the pictures will have a flashback in time to a memory as vivid as a whiff of that high-priced perfume.

Hiawatha **streamlined steam Engine No. 1 is at La Crosse, Wisconsin on May 26, 1936 taking a supply of water. Streamlined locomotives could run a few miles per hour faster than the "uncovered" steam locomotives, but they still had to make stops for fuel and water. They were sleek and pretty, but they did not engender the feelings of sentiment that those ugly brutes that looked like a steam engine did.** *C.T. Felstead*

If you are old enough to have been one of the people, including the little girl, boarding the *Hiawatha* on the Milwaukee in September, 1939, you are over the hill and approaching the Biblical three score and ten. I remember it was a wonderful time. It was a time of joy, a time of feeling safe, a time of being unhurried, a time of being certain. It was a time when you were proud and happy that you were alive and an American.

It was a time when, wanting to go somewhere, you contacted your railroad ticket agent. He figured your schedule and fare and made reservations if necessary. You did not have to find a travel agency. You were not admonished to check in one hour ahead of time. At the station you checked your baggage, up to and including trunks, and were certain when you arrived at your destination it would be there, undamaged and unpilfered.

Do you remember the white linen and polished silver, the fine food on the diners and sleeping on a Pullman? When you are crowded in that narrow airplane seat eating a warmed over in-flight meal, do you remember? *Don Heimburger collection*

This is a photo of the concourse of Union Station at Chicago and a reminder of what it was like to travel by train during World War II. Gasoline rationing was in effect, and airplanes had not yet replaced passenger trains as the means for both long and short distance travel. Travelers were predominantly from the military, for war time exigencies kept most people at home or at work in defense plants.

The display of flags from many nations was symbolic of the fact that Chicago's railroads, at that period, originated or terminated more daily passenger trains than any similar transportation hub in the world. There was supposed to be a flag for every nation, including Russia. Only those of Italy, Germany and Japan were excluded. Following the war and its concomitant disruptions and realignment of states' boundaries and identification, many of the flags were removed. *Don Heimburger collection*

Illinois Terminal Motor Car No. 300 is seen with integrated passenger carrying equipment. The passenger carrying portion was equipped with quick acting side doors for more rapid loading and unloading at metro stations. Steps were at platform level. The Illinois Terminal Railroad with its home office at St. Louis operated 339 miles of railroad in Missouri and Illinois. By 1970 Rand McNally was listing it as a "freight only" system. *Courtesy Illinois Terminal Railroad, Donald Hellman collection*

The Missouri Pacific was not unlike many other railroads. With the advent of the sleek, fast diesel-electrics that did not require servicing frequently, railroads expended large sums to provide passenger equipment that harmonized with the engines — something like a woman buying a new dress or shoes to go with the color of the new family car.

None were able, or willing to, foresee that at the end of World War II each family could afford a car that allowed them to go places fast and make intermediate stops as they desired. Likewise, they were not able to foresee that bigger and better highway buses were evolving or that airports were being constructed with federal funds and their operations subsidized.

Many railroads, including the Missouri Pacific, could indirectly trace their race into oblivion to the monies spent for passenger equipment that never paid out.

This is one of the *Eagle* trains that ran over D&RGW tracks between Pueblo and Denver. I rode it a few times and have to admit it was almost in the same class as the *California Zephyr*. The only thing it really lacked was mountain scenery. *Don Heimburger collection*

116

The Chicago & Northwestern was sort of an "Old Dog Trey" in the rail history of the Midwest. It shot-gunned nearly 12,000 miles of tracks across 11 states from Illinois to the east, Wyoming west, Wisconsin north and Missouri south.

It was a fine service-oriented road, always reliable and essentially safe, the kind of a railroad that rail buffs do not associate with glamour or name trains, but one that those living along its right-of-way classed as a good neighbor and friend. There are not many legends of derring-do attached to its building or operations that I know of but neither are there many discrediting remarks or slurs connected with it.

It was a partner with the UP in some connecting through trains similar to CB&Q - D&RGW - WP combinations. They were popular, but ended as others did when it became the "in" thing to do your traveling in your personal automobile.

Indicative of the C&NW's position in the railroad world is the fact that in 15 years of merger work for the Rio Grande and consultant studies, I was all over the area served by the C&NW, and never gave it more than cursory attention. I dimly recall being told once that it operated a left-handed railroad. In other words, where other railroads are set up with signals and facilities on the right as they are approached and the engine man is on the right side of the cab, the opposite was true on the C&NW. The statement stirred no interest with me, so I never took time to check it out, but it is that way yet today.

The artist's drawing of a streamlined steam locomotive on the C&NW shows streamers of coal or oil smoke from the stack and streamers of condensed steam from the cylinder trailing far behind while the drivers appear slightly elliptical — all to give an impression of great speed — and brings to mind a period of fallacious reasoning on railroads just shortly before dieselization.

Aerodynamics, as often happens, first came to attention following WWI when military ordinance experts accepted the fact that ballistically a pointed projectile had better performance figures than a rounded or blunt nosed one. In experiments they also established that if the rear of the projectile was given the same ogive slightly truncated, there was even more improvement in speed and flattened trajectory. *Chicago & North Western*

117

The concept of motor cars being used on low density, low revenue producing segments of track was accepted on many railroads. Some were operated as a combination unit consisting of the power section, Mail, Baggage and Express (MB&E), in a unit containing space for MB&E but with coupling devices for attaching passenger carrying cars. Very little effort was expended to make them pretty or to streamline them, except on the GM&O.

Two prime examples of these being plain utilitarian pieces of equipment were the B-15 on the Northern Pacific and the GE-15 on the Minneapolis & St. Paul. The GE-15 combination also had a name, *Albert Lea.*

The B-15 carried both U.S. Mail and Railway Express Agency business. The GE-25 was strictly a power unit and U.S. Mail Railway Post Office. During operation these units became uncomfortably hot in the interior, so they were equipped with a number of ventilators and easily opened windows.

They were equipped with couplers on the nose for switching purposes, but if they were like the experience of the D&RGW with its Budd cars, they were used more often to hook on an engine to advance them after breakdowns. *Don Heimburger collection*

Pennsylvania car No. 571470, an X-29 class, rides on 3-foot-gauge trucks at a connecting point with the East Broad Top Railroad. The car was being interchanged with this 3-foot gauge coal-hauling railroad. Business moving between two such different gauges posed a problem: either the lading had to be transferred or the trucks had to be changed.

The difference in railroad gauges between connecting lines became apparent in the very beginning of the emergence of railroads as a means of transportation. In the course of interchange of lading (or equipment) no easy or totally acceptable method was ever devised. This factor, more than any single other one, spelled the eventual doom of the Rio Grande narrow gauge. Many other rail operations involving either 29-, 36- or 39-inch gauge found it necessary, as did the Grande, to change to standard gauge or go out of business.

The most aggravated case I have read about was in Australia. I am told that at Canberra there was a focal point for rail line connections where eight different gauges converged in early day Australian rail history.

In peacetime the absence of the ability to readily interchange between roads poses serious economic burdens. In wartime to use railroads to move impedimenta was crucial. In WWII this was unusually apparent because numerous borders (points where the gauges from one country to another differed) were involved.

After the war, in an effort to find some solution, the U.S. military command devised and built some experimental diesel locomotives capable of multiple gauge operation. The D&RGW narrow gauge was given the headache involving two of these monstrosities. They were Engines No. 3000 and 4700. Both were diesels and of a boxy configuration. Engine No. 4700 was soon turned back to the Army because it simply refused to stay on the rails. Engine No. 3000 was somewhat better. After many experiments on the Farmington Branch (between Durango, Colorado and Farmington, New Mexico) it was proven almost successful, at least for war time purposes. It would have never been acceptable for day after day peacetime use.

It is imperative that, for equipment to stay on the rails, equilibrium be at the centerline of track at a given mass above the top of the rail. It is apparent that in the instance shown in the photo, thought has been given this factor by laying the two narrow gauge rails equidistant from the two standard gauge rails. This did place the narrow gauge trucks centered but it still left the factor of a safe point of rest above the rail as being questionable. Speed, while on narrow gauge trucks, would have to be slow, especially on curves or bumpy track. *Don Heimburger collection*

Some photographer has produced a miracle. He has caused NYC Engine No. 5271 with nine cars trailing to look like it is standing still. The train pictured here, the *20th Century Limited*, did not stop for anything once it began moving.

It must be carrying "green" flags for a following section as the *20th Century Limited* would not run with white flags as an "extra." Note the "drop" coupling head and twin air hoses. *Don Heimburger collection*

NYC Engine No. 5421, a 4-6-4 with disc-type driving wheels in Chicago on August 23, 1947 is attached to some passenger equipment barely seen near the lower left. It apparently is just arriving for the coal bunker is just about empty.

James Watts is rather well established as inventing the steam engine which brought on the Industrial Revolution, and the need to haul goods. The ultimate hauler of goods was the steam locomotive, which just kept getting bigger and burned more fuel. So much so that no fireman could shovel enough into the huge fireboxes. Which leads to the conclusion that the greatest invention in the railroad world was the mechanical stoker. Just look at the size of the bunker on 5421 and consider how many shovelfuls it took to get the pile down to the size remaining. *C.T. Felstead*

Great Northern Engine No. 5012 was one of two electric locomotives operated by the GN on its transcontinental line in the Cascade Mountains of Washington state. Each locomotive was 101 feet long, weighed 360 tons and developed 5,000 hp. They were designed for and used primarily to move trains on the heavy grades found in crossing the Cascade Range.

Electricity fed into the 16-axle located motors furnished the power to move the behemoth. The electricity was transmitted from overhead wires to the engine by trolley connection. The operation was bidirectional with control cabs and trolley on either end making it unnecessary to turn the engine. This was an important feature when the unit was used in helper service to boost trains to the summit then run light to the bottom of the heavy grade. *Great Northern Railway*

Although never quite in the same class as the great *California Zephyr* trains, the Great Northern streamliners always ran a close second. There was the *Empire Builder*, later renamed the *Western Star*, in transcontinental passenger service between Chicago and Seattle. The 2,211-mile route was covered in 45 hours. Burlington operated the Chicago to St. Paul segment, the Great Northern St. Paul to Seattle portion. A connecting train provided the same 45-hour schedule between Chicago and Portland.

The 12-car streamliner, powered by a two-unit, 4,000 hp diesel-electric engine, No. 504, was photographed along the Columbia River near Wenatchee, Washington. *Great Northern Railway*

Another Great Northern Railway streamliner, the *Red River*, had a shorter route and fewer cars than the *Empire Builder*, but the quality of service was on a par with its big sister. The *Red River* made a round trip daily between Grand Forks, North Dakota and Minneapolis-St. Paul. The completely new five-car train went into service in June, 1950. Great Northern Engine No. 512 was the power on the head-end. *Great Northern Railway*

Great Northern accepted the Mallet compound articulated locomotive concept for use in mountainous territory some four years earlier than the D&RGW. A representative Great Northern model was Engine No. 1800, one of five such built by Baldwin Locomotive Works and purchased by the Great Northern in 1906.

The Rio Grande put Engine No. 3361, Class L-77, 2-6-6-0, built by Alco into service in 1909. This configuration was unique and interesting to watch. Several of these were rebuilt from 0-6-6-0s. Class L-62 2-6-6-2 was built by Alco in February, 1910.

Mallets were successful from the beginning in hauling heavy tonnage up steep grades. I think they were more impressive than the ugly, smelly diesels that replaced them. *Great Northern Railway*

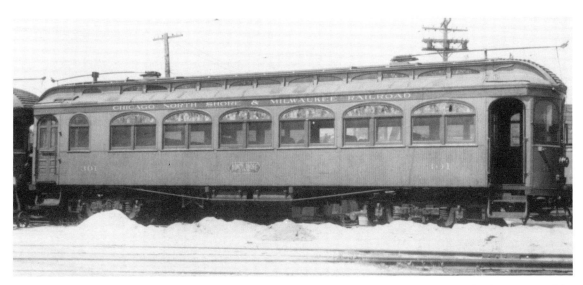

North Shore Car No. 301 at rest in a snowy yard in Chicago. It was no doubt very cold, for when there is snow on the ground in Chicago, pity the poor switchmen — and those poor people who live there.

Chicago has accomplished a lot since the Great Fire of October 8, 1871 on DeKoven Street when a cow kicked over a lantern and burned nearly the entire city, including a crossroads where, at one point, 19 railroads converged. Remarkably, in 1848 the Illinois and Michigan Canal opened, connecting the Chicago River with the Des Plaines River at Joliet, and in the same year the merchants of Chicago tried to get an ordinance passed preventing railroads entering Chicago. However, in spite of their efforts there was a railroad in Chicago by the end of 1848. *M.D. McCarter collection*

If you are old enough to remember when painting the sides of freight cars was a popular way of advertising, you are almost as old as I am. It was encouraged by traffic departments of many railroads. Car owner lines loved the practice of leasing cars to individual packers, producers or manufacturers. But the poor railroad car distributor, chief dispatcher and traffic representative suffered when any given assigned car did not make schedule on the outward bound move or on return for the next loading.

Oscar Mayer is still making wieners, and Kroger Company is selling them. Fans at spectator sports are the biggest buyers. You eat them under several designations: wieners, frankfurters, hotdogs, et al.

I questioned the spelling of wieners and went to the dictionary. Not only did I learn the correct spelling, but I learned that a frankfurter is not a wiener. The dictionary says "a wiener is usually shorter and more slender than that of a frankfurter." *Don Heimburger collection*

M&StL Engine No. 623 is going onto or backing off the turntable at Cedar Lake roundhouse in Minneapolis, Minnesota on July 11, 1938. Metropolitan land values soon made it too costly to own an area large enough for wyes to turn power as the length of locomotives increased. Increased weight and length made it necessary to constantly remodel turntables used in lieu of wyes and these, in turn, in order to handle the larger power, had to be powered. *Don Heimburger collection*

CB&Q *Silver Speed* Engine No. 9910 A&B units are enroute to be coupled to the Burlington-Rio Grande-Western Pacific *Exposition Flyer* in 1941. This was one of the earliest diesel-electrics and almost for a surety one of the first units assigned to passenger service exclusively. It was encased in shiny stainless steel.

Eight years later an improved model pulled a string of passenger cars also of stainless steel across the countryside from Chicago to San Francisco. On March 21, 1949 the *Exposition Flyer* was replaced by the most famed passenger train in the country, the *California Zephyr*.

125

A head-on shot of an EMD F unit, Engine No. 200, of the Soo Line. The Soo Line operated about 4,700 miles of railroad in Illinois, Michigan, Minnesota, and Wisconsin and as far west as Montana and the Dakotas.

Not as large as the GM&O, the Soo had almost as great and enviable a reputation for running a top notch railroad. *Norm Schreiner collection*

CB&Q Engine No. 5621, a high speed 4-8-4 locomotive was at home with either freight or passenger cars. Usually called a Northern type, this was one of the most beautiful steam engines ever built, second only to its earlier-born sibling, the Baldwin-built M-64 Class. Engine No. 5621 was of the M-68 Class. They could be differentiated by the fact that the M-68 was a bit heavier, 8' 2" longer and had disc-type drivers. The M-64 had spoked drivers.

Engine No. 5621 was either brand new or just out of the shops when this photo was taken.

Here is Wabash Engine No. 454, a road-switcher just out of the shops. It has two features that were slow in developing, although when used in switching service, were long needed.

It has two headlights. The upper one is for a strong beam while on the road; the lower of less candle power to be used while switching. On earlier models the only way to reduce the brilliance of the headlight was by employing a rheostat. When it worked it was satisfactory. When it did not or when the engineman was thoughtless and failed to set it during night operations the too bright light posed a hazardous problem to switchmen on the ground or made passing signals sometimes difficult.

The practice of using contrasting colors or patterns and designs in an effort to beautify these inherently boxy, ugly lines of the GP configurations was exceedingly costly and required great expertise in the paint shop. One break or flaw in a stripe or at the line where colors changed never failed to catch the eye and ruin the overall effect.

The other good change is the placing of the whistle (horn) on the side of the unit instead of on top of the cab. *Don Heimburger collection*

Chicago, South Shore & South Bend Engine No. 1001-1008 coupled electrics. They were no doubt efficient, but even uglier than diesel electrics. This would have been a real impressive picture if a shiny steamer had been on the point.

Ugly or not, they were real haulers. Just look at that string of pipe stretching all the way back to the horizon. A train of pipe with as many cars as this one will lay a lot of miles of pipe line that will carry billions of cubic feet of natural gas in its lifetime to keep a lot of people warm. *Don Heimburger collection*

Reading Engine No. 939 coupled to passenger equipment. This was classed as a Camelback but in some respects falls short of looking like the more commonly depicted Camelback engines. *Don Heimburger collection*

Texas & Pacific Engine No. 469, an 0-6-0, coupled to a tank car and the engine driver looking back for signals on September 19, 1948 at Ft. Worth, Texas.

Look the way that smoke is blowing almost parallel to the ground. You would easily recognize you were in Texas where the wind never stops blowing. I have never been as cold in my life as I was during the winter I spent working near Ft. Worth. *C.T. Felstead*

CB&Q Engine No. 507, a 0-6-0 at rest in the Burlington Yard at Chicago on October 7, 1939. *R.H. Kennedy, C.T. Felstead collection*

TRRA Engine No. 165, an 0-6-0, is coupled to a piece of passenger equipment probably at a switch shanty in one of the yards at St. Louis serviced by the TRRA. The engineman has his hand on the throttle just waiting for a signal. The date is December 22, 1940.

I spent about a week with the TRRA people in 1969 or 1970. I was trying to decide whether to leave the Rio Grande and accept a better paying job offered to me by TRRA. The pay was better but the perks and retirement features of the Grande were better so I said, "No, but thanks for the offer." *R.L. Fuster, C.T. Felstead collection*

Rock Island Engine No. 280, a 0-6-0 Rock Island Class S-40, at Blue Island Yard on July 4, 1947. *C.T. Felstead*

Union Pacific Engine No. 4754 in the UP yard at Denver, Colorado on July 27, 1950. *C.T. Felstead*

A manufacturer's plate for combination car destined to the D&IM. Note lettering will have to be revised and trolley added. Being a combination it may have been intended for one of several previous earlier railroads operating in Golden-Central City-Georgetown area, later consolidated in whole or part as the Denver & Intermountain Railroad Co. in 1904. The D&IM was electrified in 1909. *M.D. McCarter*

Chapter 8
Little Known Standard Gauge

A Healing Nation

The War Between the States over, the United States, including Colorado Territory, visualized what these now truly United States could best do to recuperate. Railroads as an improved means of transportation of people and goods had come to the front as one of the greater needs. In the almost totally undeveloped Colorado Territory this was especially true. Talking about railroads was the main subject of conversation. Between 1865 and about 1880 in Colorado, 88 railroads were proposed, planned, chartered, built or in the process of building. The Denver-Golden area accounted for more than 50 of these.

A number of these were actually built and operated to serve individual outlying communities or mines. Most were only a few miles long. Often their grandiose names were longer than the railroads. Not all can be listed, but those that went into the eventual emergence of the Denver and Intermountain Railroad can best be defined in

chronological order. Each that came to be a part of this system originally was built to serve a community in the sphere of Denver's influence, or, to serve a coal mine, a hard rock silver or gold mine, fire clay quarry or an agricultural area.

Originally each was steam powered and later electrified for the D&IM. When the localized, specific needs disappeared, the D&IM disappeared also. From first dream to abandonment spanned a period of 88 years. A small segment of about 5 miles from Denver to Federal Center continued to operate until recently as the Associated Railroads.

D&IM TROLLEY

The D&IM is often referred to as a narrow gauge, but it was in reality *trolley gauge*, 3'6" between the ball of the rails. This is because it began as an interurban people-moving line and all the trolleys owned were that gauge. When coal mining became such a factor that portion of the line located in the coal mining district was standard gauged, or more properly, made dual gauge between Clear Creek Junction and Golden.

The high point of activity was 1914 followed by a gradual slowdown which leveled off about 1920. Thereafter, as one coal mine after another shut down, the short spurs into the mines were abandoned.

The ownership and designation of short pieces of railroad and the relationship between owning-controlling groups coupled with frequent and rapid changes were so convoluted and directors and finance so interlocked, it would require much research to sort it all out. Once sorted out the results would require a pamphlet size book to correlate in orderly fashion. Suffice it to say, for 88 years it served the community well.

DISPATCHER'S TALE

The D&IM used the railroad Standard Book of Rules. Trains were operated by train orders and timetable schedules. The man I succeeded as Chief Transportation Officer on the Rio Grande, C.V. (Vi) Colstadt, worked for a while as a train dispatcher on the D&IM. He was fond of telling of one experience he had that showed the D&IM had one advantage in handling trains the Rio Grande did not have.

Colstadt was a man's man, but on the Rio Grande he was never known as anything but Vi. Physically, he was about the laziest man I have ever known, but mentally, he was exactly the opposite. I worked with and under Vi for many years, and it never ceased to astonish me that such an indolent man could make decisions so rapidly and appropriately and put them into action. He could absorb the details of a crisis immediately and his mind seemed to work like a computer and dictate the necessary actions just as fast.

Vi learned telegraphy under his mother at a Chicago, Burlington & Quincy station north of Denver and then went to work on the Colorado & Southern. Like most lightning slingers of the day, he like to change railroads. His next stop was the Denver & Intermountain where he soon was promoted to train dispatcher.

He next came to the Rio Grande where he worked up through the ranks along the same route that I did until he retired on the last day of May, 1966, as chief transportation officer. Upon his retirement, I assumed his position and responsibilities with the title of Assistant Vice President of Operations.

Vi and I had both put out our share of lap orders as dispatchers, although, by luck and the grace of God, none of them had ever come to an actual collision betweens trains.

One day we found ourselves discussing what action to take if a dispatcher had set up a potential collision with a lap order.

"You know," Vi said, "it would be nice if we had a set up like the one I was able to take advantage of once on the D&IM to keep two trains apart."

Of course, I was all ears and pushed him to tell his story. To understand his story, it is necessary to know that the D&IM was an electrified line, and power was controlled from a central point where a bank of switches was under the control of a trusted man around the clock. Each segment of railroad had a control switch. A master switch could be thrown that would immediately stop the flow of electricity to the entire system.

"I was taking the transfer one time when I became aware that the guy I was relieving had two passenger cars heading toward each other that were due for a cornfield meet in about 10 minutes," Vi

D&IM Engines No. 1107 and No. 1106 between Leyden and Golden, Colorado with passenger cars and a caboose. Occasionally, a train normally operating only as a passenger hauler would be lined up to stop at one of the mine tipples to do a bit of switching. In such cases a crummy was carried as part of the consist. Engines No. 1107 and No. 1106 were General Electric electrics. They had four GE 218A motors (280 hp). *M.D. McCarter collection*

continued. "There was no office between them to stop either one with a red board. I didn't take the time to tell the poor bastard what he had done. I just reached for the telephone and rang in the control man at the power plant." "When the control man answered," Vi said, "I told him 'Don't ask questions, don't argue. We'll talk later. JUST PULL THAT BIG SWITCH!"

"He did," Vi said," and then came back and informed me there now was not a damned wheel moving and that none could until he closed the master switch. I told him that was fine and to keep it that way until I personally told him to close it. Then I lined up for a messenger to go by

This photograph depicts a head on collision between two D&IM electric units between Boulder and Denver, Colorado. *M.D. McCarter*

car to deliver new orders to each train out on the line and to call in when each one had received delivery," continued Vi.

"It took some waiting until this was accomplished but when it was, I called back the control and told him to start juice back into the line. We would start running trains again," said Vi.

"I'll never forget that," said Vi. "It just seemed like it popped into my head when I saw what was due to happen — if you can't stop one then stop them all. It worked."

Vi always said it was just too bad that all railroads did not have this capability for stopping collisions.

D&IM interurban car No. 04 at Leyden, Colorado on July 11, 1944 ran route 82-83 Denver to Golden and turnaround. I never had an opportunity to ride any of these D&IM interurbans (or the freight trains). I moved to Denver on assignment in 1954. The D&IM was abandoned in 1953. *M.D. McCarter collection*

ABOVE: This is another angle of the same meeting at Clear Creek Junction (Arvada) pictured on the previous page. *M.D. McCarter*

LEFT: D&IM Engine No. 1107, handling freight cars, one passenger car and caboose meets Interurban car (train) No. 818 at Clear Creek Junction (Arvada) on July 27, 1948. In the last few years of operation the D&IM sometimes resorted to the same practices of other past railroads as business declined — it ran some mixed trains. No. 818 was one of the remaining scheduled one car (trolley) runs. *M. D. McCarter*

Denver & Intermountain Railroad Chronology

The following is a chronology of basic, pertinent dates of the Denver & Intermountain Railroad and its antecedents. The Denver Interurban must not be confused with the D&IM. The Denver Interurban had its inception with the appearance on Denver streets of horse drawn trolleys in 1870.

February 9, 1865 - Clear Creek & Colorado Railway Company chartered with three objectives:
1. Golden to Clear Creek to Central City
2. Golden to Boulder
3. Golden to Denver

1866 - Name changed to Colorado Central & Pacific Railroad. Union Pacific contributed some cash and placed five directors.

1867 - Colorado Central proposition classed a failure.

1868 - Resurrected at instigation of Union Pacific.

January 1, 1868 - Ground broken; construction started.

September 23, 1870 - Golden to Denver, 7-mile line completed. Not a direct route, it connected with Union Pacific line 6 miles north of Denver. Colorado Central - Union Pacific built into Black Hawk.

December, 1872 - Built to Floyd Hill.

September, 1872 to April, 1873 - Built Golden-Longmont.

August, 1878 - Built into Central City. By 1883 there were 20 operating coal mines in Jefferson, Boulder and Weld counties. Denver begging for fuel.

1888 - Denver, Marshall & Boulder Railroad incorporated and built to coal mines in Marshall, Louisville, Lafayette area.

1891 - Denver, Lakewood & Golden Railroad incorporated. Built from Denver to Golden direct.

1891 - Construction completed on Denver, Lakewood & Golden RR from east bank of Platte River at Denver to Golden, 14th Street.

1894 - Built Golden to Tindale Mine on Ralston Creek between Golden and Leyden, Colorado. This line washed out in 1904 and was abandoned.

1902 - Denver & Northwestern built Arvada to Leyden Junction — a 3'6" gauge. In July, 1902 the Denver, Northwestern & Pacific Railway and the Moffat Line was incorporated to build from Denver to Salt Lake City via Craig, Colorado. Its route would pass through Arvada also but it was standard gauge. It is not clear whether the two railroads were the same. The 3'6" gauge used only the name Denver & Northwestern.

1904 - Clear Creek Junction at Arvada to Golden. The 3'6" gauge was electrified.

1904 - Denver, Lakewood and Golden become Denver & Intermountain. It was electrified in 1909.

1910 - A spur was built to the Ruby Mine, a fireclay operation.

1920 - Denver, Golden & Morrison Railroad constructed.

1941 - D&IM controlled in part by the Colorado Southern; standard gauged Denver to Golden (Denver, Lakewood and Golden tracks).

1950 - Lakeside to Arvada Junction the 3'6" gauge was abandoned. Also, the Clear Creek Junction at Arvada electrified 3'6" gauge was abandoned. These two items included some Denver Tramway that was being operated by the D&IM.

1953 - All other tracks, including any standard gauge, were abandoned.

San Diego & Arizona Eastern RR

Soon after Hurricane Hazel devastated the area through which the San Diego & Arizona Eastern Railroad operated, its parent company, the Southern Pacific, petitioned to abandon it. The abandonment also involved that portion of the line running from the border through Tecate and Tijuana, Mexico on the Sonora & Baja California line.

Many interests protested the abandonment, including the San Diego Port Authority and the S&BC. I was hired by them to make a survey, estimate rehabilitation costs and project operating costs after restoration to counter SP claims.

In company with Bill Stonehouse, representing the Port Authority, and Julio Granados, representing the S&BC, the project was started on September 8, 1977 and concluded late in the spring after the hearing before the Interstate Commerce Commission and the California Public Utilities Commission. The hearing resulted in an order for restoration and continued operation, and this order was complied with.

At the opening of the hearing the SP submitted an amended estimate for restoration. Mine was tendered at the same time. After these were accepted as exhibits and we compared our figures,

I do not know who was more surprised, the SP or I, as there was only a difference of $28,000 on the bottom line. No, there was no collusion between me and the engineers. We simply made our estimates based on proven railroad engineering. The hearing examiner did question both of us very closely, however, before accepting this fact.

Because our estimates were so close, the matter of rehabilitation costs was a moot point. So, the hearing proceeded to operating costs and to several days of customers testimony.

ACCOUNTING ALTERATIONS

In the matter of operating costs, the SP and I produced estimates that were far apart. The crux of the matter was that, after acquisition, the SP continued operating the SD&AE as a separate entity within a complete corporate structure. This, of course, was costly but permitted many legal avenues for channeling SD&AE income to reflect either profit or loss as was desirable at any given period. All accounting was filed according to ICC and CPUC regulations so the SP could not be faulted for taking advantage of this. It did not make logical sense to continue to do so, however, if operation was to be continued.

San Diego & Arizona Eastern Engine No. 12, a T-56 coal-burner, rests at the San Diego engine-house on October 15, 1939. *M.D. McCarter collection*

This San Diego & Arizona Eastern Engine No. 105, a C-10, waits in Tijuana, Mexico in 1932. *M.D. McCarter collection*

San Diego & Arizona Eastern combination car No. 175 was used between San Diego and El Centro, California before passenger service was discontinued. *M.D. McCarter collection*

I presented a plan for a viable alternative that could either make the SD&AE a profitable operation or, at least, a break-even one. Apparently, the examiner was convinced because the order for restoration and operation was given.

This alternative plan suggested that operation of the SD&AE as an entity, with attendant expenses cease, and that instead it be operated as a branch of the SP, which it actually was. Maintenance of track, structures and equipment could then be more economically provided for. Income and expenses would become part of the SP whole and realistically reported.

HURRICANE DAMAGE

Hurricane Hazel blew in across Baja California and was rather mild from Tijuana to Tecate and the border. By the time we started our project, the S&BC was already back on track and providing service as far north as Tecate.

On the American side, from Jacumba through Campo and the Carrizo uplift in the vicinity of Interstate 8, the damage became progressively more severe. It was relatively minor, however, compared to what we began finding on the railroad built midway between the bottom of Carrizo Gorge and the summit of the range. From that point to Coyote Wells on the east end of the range, and in the Anza-Borrego Desert, the full force of combined wind and torrential rain had played havoc with the SD&AE track. There was no means of access between these points, and I had to cover it all on foot. It was not a pleasure hike nor was it done in a day or two.

Essentially, the SD&AE on the Carrizo Gorge segment was shelf railroad built predominantly on steep hillsides with many cross drainages. Tunnels, bridges and culverts were numerous. Roadway and structure conditions prior to the hurricane were excellent, and this had somewhat mitigated the damages, but the devastation picture, on the whole, was a railroader's hell to contemplate.

Thousands of feet of shelf either had crumbled or had been washed from under the roadbed, which permitted the rail and tie structure to fall toward the bottom of the gorge. Bridges were gone or damaged to the extent that they required full replacement. Hundreds of feet of track were buried under huge rock falls that resulted from hillside walls fracturing and collapsing. Culverts were filled or washed away, aprons destroyed and much detritus deposited at each cross drainage. It was a nightmare. To understand the extent of the damage, it must be remembered that there was little or no ground cover, only bare rock and sand.

Entering the Anza-Borrego Desert segment, where the terrain was predominantly like a sandy beach, damage included thousands of feet of roadbed and track structures washed away or buried under several feet of sand. All culverts were washed away and every single bridge, all of timber construction and some lengthy, was in unrepairable condition. It all had to be replaced.

From Coyote Wells to Plaster City near El Centro the damage was about the same as between Jacumba and Carrizo Gorge.

SELECT CONSTRUCTION

I was greatly impressed by the degree of expertise and the quality of material and workmanship that had been used in building the bridges and lining the tunnels. Nearly all the tunnels were timbered and cribbed with redwood. The timbers measured 12" x 12", and the crib lagging was of a uniform four inch thickness. The bridges, all wooden and dating from an earlier era, showed that master carpenters had built them. In fact, where undamaged segments of track remained the entire line was one to be proud of. This included the S&BC portion, also.

The most awe-inspiring structure was the one shown on page 144. It was of a later vintage than the rest of the line and was built to cross a deep gorge tributary to the main Carrizo Gorge after an earthquake closed a tunnel that originally cut through the rock at the upper end of the side gorge in question.

After walking the many miles of the Carrizo Gorge line, I quit bragging about what great mountain railroad builders our Rio Grande forefathers were.

San Diego & Arizona Eastern Engine No. 106, a
C-10, sits on October 6, 1956. *M.D. McCarter
collection*

Sonora & Baja California Engines Nos. 23027 and 23029, General Electric
engines, rest at Campeche, Mexico on July 18, 1959. *M.D. McCarter collection*

The noonday sun casts shadows through the timbers of this San Diego & Arizona Eastern trestle at Carrizo Gorge. Bill Stonehouse of the San Diego Port Authority accompanied me on this visit. This 20-gauge double-barrel shotgun was protection against the abundant rattlesnakes. Spurred out are two tanks of water in case of fire. On the hillside just above the east end of the trestle is a tank once used to store water for engine use when the SD&AE was a steam road. The glare of the bright sun shining on absolutely bare rock makes the slopes appear to be snow covered in this photo. *John Norwood*

145

The San Diego & Arizona Eastern built this high trestle around a curve. Corrizo Gorge is visible beyond the trestle. *John Norwood*

LEFT: This tall, curved San Diego & Arizona Eastern trestle was built at the tunnel portal visible in the upper right corner. There were a number of strain-gauges on the trestle that demanded frequent inspections for loose braces and timbers. *John Norwood*

This San Diego & Arizona Eastern intricate trestle in Carrizo Gorge was built when the tunnel in the upper right was drilled. An earthquake sealed the old tunnel, whose portal can be seen in the upper left corner. The old tunnel did not require a trestle. *John Norwood*

Little Rock & Western

In the aftermath of the bankruptcy of the Chicago, Rock Island & Pacific, the factories and industries located exclusively on its tracks were left without rail transportation. Some were of a nature that trucks could not adequately replace the railroad carrier.

The Ark-Kraft Paper Mill, a subsidiary of the Green Bay Packaging Corporation, was one such company. Located near Perry, Arkansas, the volume of both its inbound and outbound shipments mandated it have rail access. Most critically, it required receipt and delivery of goods at Little Rock, Arkansas with the Missouri Pacific and the St. Louis Southwestern Railway.

The Green Bay Packaging Corporation operated the Green Bay & Western and was no stranger to railroad operation. It proposed to buy the segment of the Rock Island from Little Rock, Milepost 130.5, to Perry, Arkansas, Milepost 184.2. This 53.7 miles of main line, plus the three-mile spur into their plant, was designated as the Little Rock & Western Railroad.

A feasibility study involving evaluation, rehabilitation and operation was required, and R.L. Banks & Associates of Washington, D.C. was chosen to make it. Banks solicited me to make the study and the presentation.

A meeting, attended by representatives of R.L. Banks, the LR&W and myself, was held at Little Rock on April 7, 1981. The investigation and preparation of the study kept me in the Little Rock area until the middle of May.

PRICE TOO HIGH

Essentially, what was involved was the desire of the receiver to unload a package of Rock Island liabilities on the L&RW. Not only did the deal include the segment of railroad actually required to serve the Ark-Kraft Paper Mill, it also included all the Rock Island terminal facilities in Little Rock, a monumental lift bridge across the Arkansas River and the vestigial remains of the Rock Island Hot Springs Branch. This branch 4.8 miles long served a bauxite plant. Federal studies placed the value at $3,320,700. This sum was higher than the LR&W could afford to pay and exceeded the amount for which a grant could be obtained.

The first stage was to develop what the LR&W would require: how they would rehabilitate, maintain and operate the needed line. Then we needed to correlate this information with the federal study. It was apparent that an effort was being made to saddle the LR&W with a lot of unneeded real estate, trackage and facilities. Due to its urgent nature, the initial information was based on estimates and empirical formulas. The figure we arrived at was about 45 percent of the federal figure, but it was $500,000 too high to qualify for a grant.

The second stage was to refine costs of all factors and to convince the courts that the goal was only to provide transportation for a single product from the only large industry left stranded by the Rock Island bankruptcy on a section of railroad that would otherwise be torn up. The LR&W had no need for the Rock Island terminal facilities or the massive steel lift bridge. Assuredly, it had no need for the tracks to the bauxite plant and no desire to go into a real estate liquidation or scrap iron business.

SETTLEMENT PRICE

We arrived at an acquisition figure of $1,087,431. This figure could be justified and verified, and it was acceptable to all parties involved.

This was the most difficult evaluation, rehabilitation and feasibility study I was ever involved in. During the preceding decade, maintenance had been deferred by the Rock Island, and the bookkeeping and recording of operations had suffered as much or more. Much important information was either nonexistent, complex, confused or obscure. In reviewing my worksheets to write this, I can hardly believe so much work was required for what should have been a simple study.

If the LR&W had been interested in real estate or scrap salvage, which it definitely was not, the potential net value of these two items was $3,142,872. At the time, however, the market for scrap steel was almost nonexistent, real estate was in a slump, and no other railroad was interested in buying the ultramodern one-spot repair track the Rock Island had built just previous to the Union Pacific-Rock Island merger.

FAMILIAR STRUCTURES

Three old buildings in or close to Biddle Yard particularly interested me. Built of age-softened red brick with ornate decorations, they appeared to date to the Civil War. These buildings reminded me of stories told by my great grandfather who rode with General Nathan B. Forrest for the duration of the war.

A heavy battle fought at Prairie Grove, Arkansas brought defeat to the Confederate forces. They retreated to Little Rock and took a stand to protect the capitol of Arkansas. They destroyed a bridge some miles upriver of Little Rock and then built a pontoon bridge closer to the their headquarters. My great grandfather described these headquarters and the nearby hospital as resembling these old buildings.

One of these buildings has the words "Choctaw Route" chiseled in white marble near its roof. On a second building, evidently a passenger depot, there

150

This depot in Hot Springs, Arkansas on August 7, 1970 shows a well kept, aesthetic building that complements typical Hot Springs decor. When visited again in April of 1981, the building was still in fine shape. The Budweiser bench is unusual in Arkansas. *M.D. McCarter collection*

are three marble tablets, one at each end and one over the entrance, identifying the station as "Argenta". A diligent search through history and railroad books produced no explanation of either of these. At last, information was furnished by the Arkansas Historic Preservation Program. This information will be of interest to both railroad and Civil War history buffs.

FERRY BOAT/RR LINE

When the war began, Arkansas had only 38 miles of operating railroad line. It extended from Hopefield, Arkansas across the Mississippi River to Memphis, Tennessee and on to Madison, Arkansas on the St. Francis River. Early in 1862 trains began running on a new section of track reaching from Little Rock eastward to Devalls Bluff on the White River. Throughout the war, there was a 45-mile gap between these two sections of track. To complete a trip between Little Rock and Memphis it was necessary to use steamboats and stage coaches on the portion where there was no railroad. A ferry operated from Hopefield to Memphis.

The terminal for the track which ran from Devalls Bluff to Little Rock was at a town named Huntersville. It was on the west side of the

Arkansas River opposite Little Rock. This station was later named Argenta. It eventually became known as North Little Rock. After the war the two sections of track were joined together and called the Memphis & Little Rock.

The Choctaw Route passenger station was built in 1899 by the Choctaw, Oklahoma & Gulf Railroad. It was sold in 1902 to the Rock Island. Presumably, the Rock Island also acquired the M&LR.

The Argenta passenger station was nominated to the National Register of Historic Places. Photographs of this station while under Rock Island management show large Rock Island signs covering the stone Argenta tablets. The other two old brick buildings I referred to earlier are being studied for nomination also.

During the heyday of railroad passenger trains there was a restaurant in the Argenta station, as well as the usual depot functions such as a telegraph office, general business office and a baggage room at the south end. The exterior of the building was exceptionally ornate and had much floral and fruit embellishment. The projecting cornice was decorated at regular intervals with bouquets and by muted brackets inlaid with acanthus leaves.

The dark structure in the foreground is the old Little Rock & Western Railroad yard office and division headquarters at Biddle yard in Little Rock, Arkansas on April 10, 1981. Yardmasters used the bay windows to oversee operations. Beyond the street overpass the Little Rock-Oklahoma City line turns to the right. *John Norwood*

This Little Rock & Western passenger station, located just south of the freight house, has seen better days. The block signal at the right center edge of the photograph controls the approach to MoPac crossing and lift-bridge. *John Norwood*

The freight house and freight agent's office of the Little Rock & Western displays the name Choctaw Route chiseled in white marble. It is said that during the War Between the States these buildings were used as a hospital and Confederate/Union headquarters. During reconstruction after the war, numerous short railroads were built in Arkansas and throughout the South. The Rock Island gobbled up many of them in building its rail system. Others were so insignificant and short-lived that their names and histories have been lost forever. *John Norwood*

BELOW: Rock Island lift bridge spans the Arkansas River at Little Rock on April 8, 1981. Visible in the foreground is the MoPac line to Pine Bluff. Once river traffic mandated that this bridge and signal-block control be staffed around the clock, a very expensive endeavor. To add insult to injury MoPac was senior to Rock Island at the crossing and had priority in moves which meant that RI had to pay all expenses. *John Norwood*

The interior was less ornate, but the concourse was covered. This created a semi-vault which was decorated with a terra cotta ornamental tile and heavy cornice.

The Arkansas History Commission has confirmed the fact that, after retreating from Prairie Grove, the Confederate forces of Major General Thomas C. Hindman arrived at what is now North Little Rock on December 7, 1862. They established headquarters and a hospital in Huntersville. Union forces under Yankee Major General Frederick Steele and Major General James C. Blunt attacked Hindman on September 10, 1863, and the Confederate troops were forced to retreat.

CONFEDERATE SPY

David Dodd, a 17-year-old Confederate soldier, was later captured trying to pass through Union lines. He carried a notebook inscribed with many dots and dashes. This was recognized as Morse Code, and a Union telegrapher decoded it. It contained a full and accurate report of the Union forces in Little Rock, including the location of their artillery and defenses. Dodd was hanged as a spy.

Trying to trace Arkansas railways or other Southern roads in the period from 1862 to 1870 is a study in frustration. At the beginning of hostilities there were only 6,000 miles of railroad in the entire South. These rails belonged to the short, local lines using 30-pound rail. Gauges varied from 3'6" to 4'8½", 5' and even 6'.

As the Confederate Major General Lovell retreated from New Orleans, he picked up the rail and rolling stock from a small, nameless railroad that began at Ponchatoula, Louisiana near Lake Pontchartrain. When the retreat was over he began building a new railroad. This is not as incongruous as it appears. Rails weighed only 30 pounds per yard and were 20-26 feet long. Locomotives seldom weighed over 18 tons, and cars weighed much less. They could be moved by mules or oxen, and crossties could be hacked on site.

For the balance of the war, both sides followed this pattern. When they did not, they destroyed as much as possible. On May 29, 1862, by order of military authorities, Confederate forces destroyed all railroad facilities at Corinth, Mississippi to prevent them from falling into Union hands.

A common method of destroying a rail line was to tear up the rail and then use the ties to build large fires. Rail lengths were laid across the fire until the metal reached a red-hot temperature. Each rail, which weighed 200-300 pounds, was carried to a convenient tree or rock and bent around it. It was then impossible to use the rail again.

Utah Railway: Helper to Provo

For the Rio Grande, and especially its employees stationed or working at Helper, Utah in the Carbon County coal fields, the Utah Railway was always a conundrum and, frequently, a big headache. In our relations with the Utah, we never knew for certain if we were dealing with an entity or an appendage. Was there really a Utah Railway, or was it the alter ego of our long-time adversary, the Union Pacific?

Locally, our problems stemmed from the manner in which the Utah operated their trains between the Helper and Provo, Utah terminals. There was a double track between these points, and the Utah owned the eastbound track from Provo to Thistle, a distance of 20.62 miles. The rub was that, under the trackage agreement, the Utah had equal operating rights even though the Rio Grande dispatched and maintained everything in the district.

OVERLOADED ALCOs

The Utah's philosophy of train operation was to load their engines, which were downgraded Alcos in the 1950s, to the limit they could pull. The Utah had to obtain authority from the Rio Grande dispatchers in order to enter the main track at the Utah Railway Junction, so we had quasi-control up until then. Once they were out on the westbound track heading for Soldier Summit, however, the headaches began. The Utah was satisfied with a speed of as little as five mph for their coal trains up the mountain. The Rio Grande operated at 15-20 mph to Colton and more to the summit.

The old, poorly-maintained Alcos moaned and groaned up the 2-2.4 percent grade to Kyune, a 12.5 mile trip. The Utah did not make any noticeable effort to go much faster on the 1.10 percent grade on the remaining 5.6 miles to Soldier Summit. We did not have Centralized Traffic Control capability to use the double track to advantage in passing the Utah trains, so we just had to follow the Utah's slow trains, cuss and sweat it out. The situation was the same eastbound with the Utah's empty trains moving from Provo to Utah Railway Junction.

DOUBLE TRACKING

The Rio Grande began a program of double tracking in order to accommodate the coal movement from Carbon County mines over Soldier Summit as early as 1897 when it laid double track from Soldier Summmit to Detour. In 1921-22 a more favorable route was constructed between Soldier Summit and Gilluly, and double track was extended to Thistle. This then mandated extension on to Provo. The Utah had already built track

Utah Railway Engine No. 202, an oil burning 2-8-8-2, shows a tipple dating back to the days of coal burners. URY was a stepchild of the Union Pacific. This photograph was taken in September of 1938 but by the time I was Helper trainmaster in June of 1953, the URY was using a fleet of downgraded Alcos. They were noisy, stinky, slow and fouled the ballast with leaking oil. *M.D. McCarter collection*

from Provo to Thistle. A contract and agreement between the two lines incorporated this trackage into the double tracking program.

On the east side, the first segment of double track from Colton to Soldier Summit was laid in 1906, Helper to Castle Gate and Kyune to Colton was laid in 1909, and Castle Gate to Kyune was laid in 1912. By 1914, including the Utah segment, there was double track from Helper to Provo except for a single track gauntlet between Colton and Soldier Summit in later years.

Settlement of Rio Grande-Utah bills was a constant matter of contention. Locally, it was not the Rio Grande's problem. There was one other problem, however, that threatened both roads and could have resulted in Interstate Commerce Commission violations calling for heavy fines. Only extreme measures taken jointly by the two roads corrected the situation, and these required discretion and no fanfare on the part of the local officers, union representatives and the individuals involved.

There was an extremely heavy demand for coal from Carbon County between 1950 and 1955. Some mines worked extra shifts and Saturdays. Both the Utah and the Rio Grande were running trains as fast as power and crews were available. At Helper, switch engine assignments were increased to keep up with the added work of sorting out and making up additional empty trains to send to the mines where they were loaded as fast as they were set at the tipples. The concept of unit coal trains had only begun to be thought of as being possible.

DOUBLE DIPPING

Seldom can anything be kept quiet on a railroad. In the beanery or switch shanty, railroaders are inclined to do a lot of talking and bragging. From some of these brags, word got out that a number of train and engine service crews, switchmen and shop men were making considerable extra money working for both the Rio Grande and the Utah. A few used different names, but they mostly used their own and were building seniority on both roads in their respective service. They were also playing the "first-in-first-out" game on both call boards by laying off on one railroad or the other for a trip or two if necessary.

A private investigation by Rio Grande and Utah officials determined that this situation was widespread and being condoned by the local union representatives, some of whom were playing the game also. The individuals involved were increasing their earnings but creating hazards and violations. In frequent cases, a man might not get any sleep or rest for 24 hours or more and was, thus, not mentally alert. Potential accidents were just waiting to happen.

The flagrant violations of the 16-Hour Act were as dangerous as the potential accidents that the fatigued train and engine service people could cause. A man could come in from a run on either of the railroads, report in on the other and almost immediately be called for duty. Seldom did these workers get even a three-hour break. For example, a man could serve maybe 10 hours of duty on the Rio Grande, report in on the Utah and be called out for a trip on that line from Martin to Provo. This trip could take from eight to 12 hours. Not counting the lack of a three-hour break, the man, upon arrival in Provo, would have been on duty a total of 20 hours under provisions of the 16-Hour Act. In this example, the Utah would be held responsible for the violation along with the man. If the situation was reversed the Rio Grande would be responsible.

Meticulous checking by the two roads produced a list of the names of those who were guilty. These men, accompanied by a union representative, were called to closed-door sessions where it was clearly defined that they could have only one employer and one seniority. The 16-hour Act was explained, as well as the penalties involved for violation.

The practice ceased immediately. Some Utah employees opted to become Rio Grande employees while some Rio Grande men stayed with the Utah. Each man made his decision based on where he thought he would benefit the most.

Utah Railway left D&RGW tracks at Utah Railway junction 2.4 miles west of Helper, Utah, and ran one mile to Martin. A second track maintained and operated by the D&RGW but owned by the Utah Railway ran 20.62 miles from Thistle to Provo. Here Utah Railway Engine No. 101, a 2-10-2 oilburner, heads into the Martin terminal on September 6, 1950. *M.D. McCarter collection*

Butte, Anaconda & Pacific

Around the mid-1950s, while I was assigned to the Utah end of the Rio Grande, I took the opportunity to spend a brief visit with my sister and her husband at Butte, Montana. My brother-in-law was employed by the Anaconda Copper Company in a capacity that gave him the freedom and opportunity to become well-acquainted with the operation of the Butte, Anaconda & Pacific Railway, and he spent two days showing me around.

MEMORABLE UNDERGROUND

This was an efficient operation above ground with highly-maintained tracks and equipment. Underground, the railroad was even more remarkable. As I remember, there were 128 miles of underground railroad. It was electrified and dispatcher controlled with Centralized Traffic Control.

The open pit operation at Butte, Montana used immense machinery and trucks to bring the ore out of the pit. Some of these trucks had the same power application system as diesel-electric locomotives. An engine ran a generator that produced power that was transmitted to an electric motor located at each corner of the rig. One of the shovel buckets was so large that as it sat with its scoop on the ground, I was able to drive my automobile into it with space left over.

As I watched the ease of handling, silent operation and pulling power of the electrified motors, I could only wonder why, over the years of railroad development, electrification had not been pursued more. I was familiar with all the reasons given by railroads, but I was still impressed.

Butte, Anaconda & Pacific combine No. 11 at Butte, Montana waits to make a shift change on September 4, 1950. It made the commuter run from Butte to Anaconda carrying miners. Stations along the line included Butte, Durant, Anaconda and Brown. *M.D. McCarter collection*

Butte, Anaconda & Pacific Engines No. 65 and 66 with combine No. 11, seen here on September 4, 1950, were used to transport Anaconda Copper workers between Butte, Montana and working sites of the copper company in the area. *M.D. McCarter collection*

Engines No. 50 and 51 pull a train of copper ore from Anaconda, Montana to Butte on a Butte, Anaconda & Pacific electrified line. This private line owned by Anaconda Copper Co. to haul ore from pits had a total mileage of 116. It connected with Union Pacific, Milwaukee and Burlington but mainly handled only the copper company's business. *John Norwood*

Electrified Butte, Anaconda & Pacific Engines No. 65 and 66 coupled to combine No. 11 at Butte, Montana are ready to leave on a change of shift commute run to Anaconda on September 4, 1950. *M.D. McCarter collection*

Missouri & Arkansas

One week after my father's 16th birthday, July 31, 1909, he went to work as an agent/telegrapher for the Missouri & Arkansas Railway. As a raw beginner, he was sent to Arlburg, a small station in Arkansas on the Little Red River.

This town was more than just small. It could barely be called a community. The residents made their living cutting oak trees into barrel bolts. The M&A hauled these north to be converted eventually into kegs used by distillers to hold whiskey. Most families ran a small still on the side to take care of the family refreshments.

NOSTALGIC DAD

After he retired, Dad began a determined campaign to induce me to take him back down through the area he had not forgotten in all of his boomer career. He kept talking about the fine fishing in the Little Red River, squirrel and turkey hunting and the beautiful open groves of hardwoods on the hillsides that the natives cut to make barrel bolts. He remembered how the groves were so clear of underbrush that the bolts were loaded on skips or sleds and brought to the loading point on the M&A using oxen for power.

I insisted that it would not be the same 50 years later, but he still wanted to go see for himself. As I had read many tall tales about the incredible trout fishing on the White River, I finally agreed to take him on the condition that we would float the White River first.

My dad, my wife and I drove the camper to Norfolk, Arkansas, a short distance from the Norfolk Dam. We then hired a native guide and his john-boat, a double-ended flatboat, and floated the White River down as far as Sylamore, Arkansas for several days. The fishing was everything that had been said of it. I did run into one problem, however. I forgot that Arkansas was Local-Option, and it was practically impossible to buy either legal or illegal whiskey. I kept after our guide, but he refused to produce. On the afternoon that we paid him, I gave him a $20 tip and a fine pocketknife he had admired constantly. That evening we went to the only restaurant in Norfolk. On our return, we found a flat bottle bearing no marks and without an explanation propped up near the camper door. It was as clear as spring water and about as fine a sipping liquor as I have ever tasted.

We left Norfolk and more or less followed the line of the White River Division to Flippin, Arkansas, a town where we had resided for a short time while Dad worked for the Missouri Pacific after our return from his Colorado tour on the Denver & Rio Grande Western-Rio Grande Southern as an agent/telegrapher. We then went

Missouri & Arkansas Railway Engine No. 15, a 2-6-0, stands in the midst of other discards at Harrison, Arkansas on May 7, 1949. Note that the siderods are still connected. *M.D. McCarter collection*

At age 16, in 1909, my father began his career as a "boomer" telegrapher on the Missouri & Arkansas Railway. Here Engine No. 18, a 4-6-0, rests at Harrison, Arkansas on May 5, 1949.

At Butte, Montana I was impressed by the capabilities of electrification on a railroad both above ground and underground. While I was in Butte, the Anaconda Copper Co. had converted to the use of huge trucks to haul ore out of the Butte pit. The Kennecott Copper Co. in Bingham, Utah, not far from Salt Lake City, ran tracks and trains into and out of its pit. Electrification was used here also and, as at Butte, the tractive effort and efficiency of these locomotives was impressive. *M.D. McCarter collection*

A 2-6-2 Engine No. 250 in motion on the Bonhomie & Hattiesburg Railroad.

Its home office was at Fernwood, Missouri. At Hattiesburg it connected and interchanged with the Southern and Illinois Central then ran east 27 miles to Beaumont, Missouri where it met and interchanged with the GM&O. It was a freight only belt line and still operated in the 1970s. *Don Heimburger collection*

on to Harrison, Arkansas. We looked around, but I don't recall seeing any railroad structures or set-aside equipment. Apparently, there were some when the pictures of the M&A Engines #15 and #18 were taken in 1949.

FINALLY FOUND

Our maps did not show a place named Arlburg, however, Dad insisted that there had been such a town. Finally, an old-timer we met confirmed its existence and gave us directions on how to find the location, which was about all that was left. Only one building, a two-storied, weathered frame

structure, still remained, and Dad said it was the boarding house he had lived in. Although it was in sorry shape, it was still being used as a county orphanage. The balance of the area had been reclaimed by nature.

ELUSIVE BASS

We found a track leading to the Little Red River and finally broke away enough undergrowth to camp for the night. I rigged up and went down to the river to catch us a mess of those big bass Dad had told us about. By the time my wife blew the horn for supper I had caught one scrawny tur-

162

Millions of board feet of lumber for decades came from the immense stands of timber of the Northwest. Logs to be converted to lumber were cut by crews such as this one of the "MC Log Co" and moved to mills by logging railroads such as the Blackhills Northern Railway Co. This picture was taken in 1907 at a logging location somewhere in the Blackhills stand of timber in Washington state. *George Cummings collection*

TOP LEFT: Columbus & Greenville No. 506, a 2-8-2, is westbound near Indianola, Mississippi in May of 1946. *R.W. Richardson*
BOTTOM LEFT: Columbus & Greenville No. 501 enters Columbus, Mississippi on March 10, 1944. *C.W. Witbeck*

tle. The following day was better. I caught two turtles.

No chattering squirrels or gobbling turkeys greeted the sun to awaken us. The fine oak, hickory and walnut trees had all been cut, and where they had stood, open and regal, sassafras, sumacs and blackberries fought for existence in the tangle of devil's whip, a thorny vine that reclaims the Ozark Mountain cutover land with miles of impenetrable vines and millions of flesh- tearing thorns.

Dad had originally wanted to return via Pittsburgh, Kansas; Joplin, Missouri; and a few other places where he had worked. What he saw at Arlburg, however, caused him to finally say, sadly, "I guess you should never try to return to remembered places. You can only be disappointed. Let's head for home."

Chapter 9
Linking East with West

World Trade

The mid-1800s saw world trade flourishing, and there was a universal demand for a shorter route for moving goods from the East and the West, between Asia and America and Europe. The Suez Canal, which opened in November of 1869, cut the distance from Bombay to London from 12,352 miles to 7,321 miles by eliminating the need to go around the Cape of Good Hope. This benefitted England and Europe, but the Western Hemisphere was also demanding faster means of interactive trade with Asia and the Orient.

Completion of the Central Pacific-Union Pacific transcontinental railroad only partially solved the problem. The AT&SF started west through the southern corridor. The Great Northern and Northern Pacific projected in the northern corridor.

MISLEADING MAPS

As early as 1870 railroad tycoons and developers began looking for a shorter land route between the Atlantic and the Pacific. Chicago, Kansas City and St. Louis were accepted as the focal points from which new railroads to Pacific ports were projected. Flat maps give a distorted projection of distances that produce anomalies. A flamboyant railroad developer, Arthur Edward Stillwell, was aware of this.

In actual distance he calculated it was 400 miles closer from Kansas City to the excellent Pacific port of Topolobampo, Sinaloa, Mexico than it was by the CP-UP or other projected route. Central and South American ports were closer to Kansas City than San Francisco by 400 miles.

In 1886 the 27-year-old go-getter helped promote a belt railway network at Kansas City. Next came the Kansas City, Pittsburgh and Gulf, the predecessor of the Kansas City to deepwater ports on the Gulf of Mexico. The route chosen was "as straight as the crow flies." This term, first used by Stillwell in his promotions, later and for many years was the slogan of the KCS.

Financed mostly by English and Dutch money, the line was started in 1893. Because of excessive ambition, Stillwell overextended and his balloon burst. The "cannibals" of Wall Street and "Bet-a-Million Gates" took over.

RESURRECTED DREAM

A promoter with drive and ambition does not let one failed scheme bury him. In 1900, still a pusher and planner, Stillwell, then 41, resurrected the long-discussed dream of a railroad from Kansas City to Topolobampo. His version of the line was an entrepot for grain and manufactured goods from the United States to Asia and India. Reciprocally, products from the East would move to American markets. His design was for a railroad 1,600 miles long from Wichita, Kansas, and Kansas City to Topolobampo.

The railroad which he named the Kansas City, Mexico and Orient was to be routed southwest across Oklahoma Territory to Sweetwater and San Angelo, Texas then to the Rio Grande River. Crossing the river into Chihuahua the line would continue southwesterly across the Sierra Madres del Oriente mountain range and along the Rio el Fuerte to Topolobampo.

Stillwell raised sufficient money from Kansas City businessmen and English investors to build from Wichita to San Angelo. Starting at the Pacific Ocean end he built from Topolobampo, up through the fertile El Fuerte Valley to the foot of the Sierra Madres del Oriente. Short segments of railroad were also built east and west from the city of Chihuahua. By 1907 interest in the project almost died. Stillwell was one of the few still interested in it and because of his interest the disjointed segments of the KCM&O were barely kept operating.

TWO FORECLOSURES

Revolution in Mexico nearly caused a complete shutdown of business in Mexico. The Mexican segments were destroyed to a great extent by revolutionists. In the United States the profits of operations became nonexistent and capital investment terminated. Bankruptcy became inevitable. The KCM&O went into receivership in 1912 and was still there in 1928. The line was extended by the receivers from San Angelo to Alpine, Texas, but could go no further. The line was first foreclosed in 1914. World War I came along but the U.S. Railroad Administration found no use for the line. It was foreclosed a second time in 1924.

The receiver was William T. Kemper. His task was somewhat lightened when oil was discovered and developed in KCM&O territory. In 1927 the picture was bright enough for Kemper to approach several major railroads: SP, MoPac, Rock Island, CB&Q and the ATSF.

The AT&SF realized the KCM&O, if bought by another major railroad, could make for strong competition in the south Texas plains.

At the time the Orient operated 735 miles in the U.S. and 320 miles in Mexico. It owned 75 steam locomotives most badly in need of repairs, 1,404 freight cars and 32 passenger cars. Light rail and deteriorated ties were laid on a roadbed that was in very poor condition. To keep any major competitor from buying the line, AT&SF offered Kemper $14 million. He accepted in 1928.

LOST LINE AGAIN

One year later AT&SF sold the Mexican segments to B.F. Johnson, a sugar planter in Siniloa. The price was $600,000 in cash and a $900,000 mortgage. He defaulted on the mortgage, and in 1940 the line was acquired by Mexico.

The KCM&O was rehabilitated by the AT&SF and the line extended to Presidio, Texas on the Rio Grande River. A branch was built from San Angelo to Sonora, Texas. Agricultural products picked up along the KCM&O route; AT&SF made some improvements and incorporated portions of the line in their main freight operations in a way that saved as much as 285 miles on some traffic.

The Mexican government was also making improvements on its segments and began closing the gaps to provide a line from Presidio to Topolobampo. The program was completed in November, 1961 at a cost of $88 million.

I had heard and read that the building of the railroad across the Sierra Madres del Oriente mountains was a engineering feat that had to be seen to be believed.

In March, 1973, my wife and I flew to Mazatlan, Mexico, to begin a jaunt along the west coast of Mexico by third class Mexican buses. You have never really seen a country or got acquainted with its inhabitants until you go third class.

Eventually we reached Los Mochis, Siniloa, Mexico after jumping from town to town by bus and touring the vicinity of each one by hiring a local driver to take us to points of interest not usually seen by tourists.

ZEPHYR VARNISH

One evening returning from such a tour of the El Fuerte Valley, a fertile, productive truck vegetable area where the greater part of America's winter vegetables come from, I saw a string of "varnish" that looked like *Zephyr* equipment. The driver informed me that it was the Chihuahua al Pacifico Ferro Carillo Railroad daily westbound passenger train. Inquiries at the hotel in Los Mochis caused my wife and I to ride it. We had plenty of time and money. Later, after having my pocket picked in Culiacan, Mexico I had more time than money.

To round out our train ride, we arranged for a Mexican rancher to meet us at Creel, summit of the mountain range, and take us by four-wheel drive automobile to his ranch at the bottom of Barranca del Cobre, or Copper Canyon, headwaters of the Rio el Fuerte and "Grand Canyon of Mexico." This was the highlight of our trip. The cook was a Yaqui Indian woman who was as wide as she was tall. In addition to cooking very savory Mexican-style food, she mixed the best martinis that ever tickled my palate.

The evening before we were to return to Creel to catch the westbound train, she broiled some T-bones that weighed well over a pound each. They were simply luscious, but we paid for eating them. Very shortly after reaching our hotel in Los Mochis we both began to experience stomach cramps. Have you ever suffered Montezuma's Revenge? If in Mexico, I hope you do not.

We took turns using the one toilet in our room for a couple of hours. Finally, I thought it would be safe to go to a *farmacia* (pharmacy). I bought two large bottles of Kaopectate and returned to the hotel. We each drank a bottle in lieu of our evening meal. The anti-diarrhea preparation was effective and come morning we continued our bus riding.

Riding the Chihuahua al Pacifico through El Fuerte Valley is hardly an exciting experience. We did not go beyond the mountains to ride the portion through the desert land of Chicuahua. It too is reported to be rather boring. All of this changes when the foothills and the principal cordillera of the Sierra Madres is reached and the climb to the summit begins.

MARIGOLD VALLEY

El Fuerte Valley is one immense truck garden and very green where it is irrigated. In an area near the foothills there was a parcel of land possibly two miles by two miles that was a mass of orange color. This was where an important crop is grown: marigolds. Their blossoms are harvested

One of many high steel trestles over deep cross drainages on the Chihuahua al Pacifico is seen here. All of the trestles had this double guardrail feature. Water barrels like those at the center and far end of this trestle were kept filled religiously as fire protection in this extremely arid terrain. *John Norwood*

Engine No. 808 pulls a passenger train at Chihuahua al Pacifico's Diversadero, Mexico station. My tour of this road was behind two units of Alco power pulling a train of retired *Texas Zephyr* cars. Building and operating this line was a feat greater than that encountered on the D&RGW or the WP&Y. *M.D. McCarter collection*

at their peak, dried and shipped to large poultry farms in the U.S. to be fed to chickens to produce the uniform deep color of egg yolks we are familiar with. Some undergo a process of color extraction to be used in food coloring.

Except for Los Mochis, the only sizeable other town is at El Fuerte, originally an ancient stronghold or fort in the very early days of Mexican development. Some of the brick walls still carry marks of cannonballs fired during the numerous revolutions. In outlying environs families appear to live more or less in separate groups as squatters. Each is near some source of water and each dwelling is like the others. They consist of an open living area with a roof of brush. In this area is a stone fire ring with a top of flattened steel. At one side, always on the side struck by winds from the west, is a windowless room used for storage and protection during rain or high wind storms. It is built of wattles plastered with mud.

There were frequent small groups of similar such dwellings along the tributary of the Rio el Fuerte the railroad follows. The terrain is dry and rugged. Within a few miles after entering the foothills automobiles or roads are no longer visible. Transportation is limited to the railroad. The same is true for traveling, except for the numerous trails where men and women carry loads on their backs and burros carry loads bigger than they are. Leaving the foothills and reaching the true cordillera, the collections of huts are separated more widely; the trails become fewer and only a few people are seen.

All through these rugged, steep sided mountains and gorges are exposed rock formations and a sparse growth of shrubs. Grass is seldom seen, and deciduous trees are limited to a few cottonwoods at the bottom of canyons. Occasionally in the chaparral are copses of cedars or stunted pines. There were numerous varieties and shapes of cacti. When we were there, these cacti were masses of brilliantly hued blossoms. Other splashes of color came from widely scattered shrubs that approached tree size and whose bright orange blossoms were like a large globe in configuration.

The railroad from the foothills to the summit is essentially a shelf railroad. Many tributary gorges, some of great depth, have been spanned by numerous open deck steel trestles. Cribbing and stone walls used to provide a shelf in lieu of blasting are numerous and often extensive. Their extent and workmanship make similar structures on the Silverton Branch of the Rio Grande and on the White Pass & Yukon look like kid stuff. This is not to disparage the engineering and difficulties of building either of these, but the problems and construction requirements in building the railroad line across the Sierra Madres were simply monumental.

SMOOTH AS GLASS

The final result, and its maintenance since completion, is excellent. The roadbed is so smooth you can imagine you are on the *California Zephyr* speeding across the Utah desert. This sensation is further heightened because the equipment is old *Zephyr* cars obtained from the Colorado & Southern - Ft. Worth & Denver when these roads quit operating their *Texas Zephyrs*. I must admit that the interiors were not as clean as they once were. The kitchen car, dining car and food preparation left a great deal to be desired in cleanliness. We had been warned and thus carried our own food. The toilets had been converted to the stove pipe discharge mode, i.e. they dumped direct onto the roadbed with no water flush. Toilet tissue was provided but only in an emergency would one use them, effete Americans that is.

To augment the smoothness of a ride over perfectly maintained track was the superb control of braking and slack action by the Mexican *maquinistas - conductores de locomotor* (engineers).

The train load was good. There were few empty seats, but the American tourists, possibly railfans, numbered less than a dozen. One of them touted the White Pass & Yukon Railroad to me so in 1976 we rode it. This accounts for the only two times I was a railfan.

The steep hillside had to be excavated to make room for this Chihuahua al Pacifico passenger-freight station and side track. A community of 25-30 dwellings lies in the canyon below where there is but a trickle of water. *John Norwood*

167

Chapter 10

Mergers, Acquisitions and Abandonments

Mergermania

Beginning early in the 1960s and continuing into about the mid-1970s a fever swept the Western railroads. It can best be termed "Mergermania." There was an urgency to either be the instigator or partner in a merger. If not that, then there was the fear that you would be the victim.

The epidemic started with Burlington's application to put the BN, GN, NP, C&S and FW&D together as a system. Most railroads, for some reason, did not become too concerned about this move and opposition was light. By the time of the second hearing there was concern as testified to by the roads who now opposed the merger. It was too late. The BN became an entity blessed by the ICC.

This was the first merger case I worked. It proved to be the most punishing, physically and mentally, because the Rio Grande got involved

Belt RR of Chicago is at Clearing yard in Illinois on January 7, 1939. *Paul Eilenberger*

Burlington Route Ft. Worth & Denver Engine No. 404, a 2-8-2, pulls into Wichita Falls, Texas in the fall of 1955. *M.D. McCarter collection*

This photograph of Chicago, Burlington & Quincy-Illinois Central Interlocking Tower at Mendota, Illinois was taken October 4, 1968. *M.D. McCarter collection*

late. Unlike the 25,000 plus pages that would spew out of the UP-RI recording of the proceedings, the BN transcript was much less. Because the Grande and other roads had not entered the original hearing, copies of this transcript could only be obtained at the ICC in Washington, D.C. The Commission would not make copies and denied applicants the privilege of machine copying it. It did permit reading of the file copy and the taking of notes.

Try reading a few thousand pages of transcript on a crash bases, eight hours a day for 10 days and sorting the wheat from the chaff. Toward the end your eyes ache and your fingers become fixed in the position used in holding a pencil.

There were a few compensations. With so many people there either feeding at the public trough or on expense accounts, there is no dearth of fine eating and drinking establishments. My co-worker, R.L. (Bob) Jacobsen and I took full advantage of these and our expense accounts in the evenings.

BRAVING THE ELEMENTS

The sojourn in Washington was in no way as taxing as the inspections and overflights of the proposed BN lines which took me from amid warm rain showers to marrow freezing temperatures in St. Paul, not to mention an atmosphere almost as chilly at the headquarters of the Burlington, to Duluth-Superior where the surface temperature was even lower. Taking pictures from an airplane one thousand feet above the railroad and dock areas was inhumanly cold. The pilot, when appraised of an area we desired to photograph, would circle, then come over with wings perpendicular to the ground so I could take pictures from the door. The door had been removed before taking off. The low temperature, had you been stationary, was bad enough,

Chicago, Burlington & Quincy No. 9967 rolls the *California Zephyr* through Mt. Pleasant, Iowa on August 5, 1969 heading for home at Chicago. *M.D. McCarter collection*

Burlington engine, the *Silver Chief*, pulls a string of "old-style" and streamlined cars. *M.D. McCarter collection*

Burlington Route, Ft. Worth & Denver Engine No. 458, a 2-8-2, passes through Wichita Falls, Texas in the fall of 1955. *M.D. McCarter collection*

This Great Northern Engine No. 3394, a 2-8-2 oil burner, is at Devil's Lake, North Dakota in September, 1954. *M.D. McCarter collection*

Northern Pacific 2-8-2's like this Engine No. 1561 hauling freight near Clear Lake, Minnesota on July 15, 1953, were much smaller than the Great Northern 2-8-2's. *M.D. McCarter collection*

Here is a street-side view of Union Station in St. Louis, Missouri on July 13, 1979. About 1967 or 1968 I was offered the job of running the Terminal Railroad but turned it down. I was enjoying my assignment on the Union Pacific-Rock Island merger. *M.D. McCarter collection*

but the slipstream brought the mercury all the way to the bottom. What men won't endure for a paycheck, a challenge or the pure excitement of an occasion!

Coinciding with this project, Rio Grande management was exploring the possibility of acquiring the C&S-FW&D-BRI line. Preliminary negotiations were underway. The inspection and study of this rail mileage was under very different weather and working conditions. Wendover, Wyoming, to Denver was not too bad. It was a different story once on the FW&D into northern New Mexico and through Texas to Galveston. It was hot, blistering hot, and there is no air-conditioning on railroad Hy-Railers.

Galveston erased all the bad vibes about Texas. There was a shaded patio fronting on the Gulf of Mexico, cooled by a sea breeze, accentuated by a succession of tall, frosted drinks and dozens of freshly caught prawns served in a variety of Cajun dishes.

NO WAY OUT

By the summer of 1971 the handwriting was on the wall. The UP-RI merger for all practical purposes was a lost cause. Everyone involved, including the UP, was heartily sick of the farce. Lawyers and expert witnesses were decimating treasuries, and there were no indications when it would end. There was a common search going on among all participants for an honorable way out without losing face.

It did not require a necromancer to see that there was only one ultimate solution: the Rock Island had to enter bankruptcy. This eventually happened.

The Rock Island apparently realized and accepted this ahead of others. All maintenance except emergency ceased. The La Salle Street show place in Chicago closed, and an affordable headquarters was established in Kansas City. No longer could you delight your eyes looking at Hollywood starlets.

Chicago, Milwaukee, St. Paul and Pacific Engine No. 93A, F7A powers through Fox Lake, Illinois on July 31, 1966 with a train of Milwaukee double-deck commuter cars. Fox Lake is about 45 miles from Chicago Union Station. *M.D. McCarter collection*

ABOVE: Milwaukee Engine No. 100A is coupled with a second "A" unit and passenger train at Calumet, Michigan on October 18, 1967. *M.D. McCarter collection*

LEFT: This snow-covered Chicago, Milwaukee, St. Paul & Pacific track is about 20 miles from Newport, Washington on February 1, 1979. It was too cold a day with too poor conditions to be evaluating a railroad. *John Norwood*

MKT Engine No. 397 waits at Chetopa, Kansas for a highball to get the southbound *Katy Flyer* rolling on June 14, 1942. By the time I did any work on MKT during merger studies, steam had disappeared. *Robert Kennedy, Jr.*

Alton Engine No. 5268 with No. 14 passenger fogs through Romeoville, Illinois on July 15, 1940. Alton was classed as a switching line, but the fact remains it operated some pretty fine strings of varnish. *Vernon Scaver*

MKT Engine No. 378 with southbound *Katy Flyer* thumbs its nose at one of *Katy's* upstart diesels in Kansas City, Missouri in September of 1950. *Harold Stirton*

The Rock Island shared the Rio Grande terminal at North Yard in Denver, and we were in an enviable position to keep advised of their circumstances. Transcontinental schedules that Rock Island was part of almost ceased to exist because they could not make them. West of Belleville, Kansas, there were numerous speed restrictions, many as low as 25 mph.

Rio Grande Chief Engineer Ed Waring and I made a spot check of the line by automobile. West of Belleville there were sections we thought hardly safe for 25 mph.

The Golden Gate in San Francisco for a century was the lodestone that kept pulling the thoughts of the Rio Grande westward. However, as transcontinental competition grew through the Central Corridor it became more easily perceived that reaching the Golden Gate meant nothing if the Grande did not own or control rail lines with access to Kansas City-St. Louis and Chicago.

HIGHWAYS DEVELOPED

The Rock Island was an agrarian railroad. From its incipience as a railroad in about 1870 it was oriented to the farmer and grazier. By 1900 it was a colossus spread over the Midwest. By whatever means necessary it had acquired thousands of miles of short railroads serving prosperous farm communities. World War II brought about great improvements in size and performance of trucks. With the war over, these trucks took to the highways, and roadways were built, at taxpayer's expense, to accommodate them. Farmers and graziers soon recognized the benefits inherent in transportation coming direct to their point of production.

Once active and profitable spurs and branches of the Rock Island now had only an occasional car or two to be hauled. The tax burden went on nevertheless, and the Rock Island stopped making any effort at maintenance. Either because it was optimistic of a return to better times, or because it suffered from managerial incompetence, a realistic and active program of abandonments was not instituted. By the time the UP-RI Merger began, it was too late. The Rock Island was an anachronism, an aged behemoth whose time had come to die.

PARCEL OFFERED

From a few brainstorming sessions came an idea that when the Rock Island went bankrupt, consensus being that this was a foregone conclusion, the courts might sell in parcels rather than as an entity. If this were true then it might be possible to buy the main line to Council Bluffs and

Monon Engine No. 577, a 2-8-2, blows off steam as it hauls a string of freight southward through Lafayette, Indiana on a still day in 1938. *Paul Eilenberger*

BELOW: Monon Engine No. 571, a 2-8-2, hauls a northbound freight train over the PRR crossing at Limedale, Indiana on a "clear board" in August of 1946. No doubt the towerman was cussing the fireboy that caused such a heavy smoke. *Harold Stirton*

Chicago Outer Belt Line EJ&E No. 549 is on a caboose hop at Hegewisch, Illinois. I am constantly amazed that these 0-8-0's apparently operated satisfactorily and stayed on the rail through turnouts. *Paul Eilenberger*

BELOW: On August 26, 1946 Engine No. 431 brings the southbound *Day Express* to a halt at Monon, Indiana. About 1971 I spent a week on the Monon making a quick inspection related to a feasibility study for possible acquisition. *Harold Stirton*

What a sleek, beautiful thing this B&O Engine No. 5360 was. This 4-6-4 pulls the *Capitol Limited* by Roby Street, Chicago in July of 1937, the month and year I began my career on the Rio Grande. *Paul Eilenberger*

BELOW: B&O Engine No., 5233, a 4-6-2, is outward bound from Chicago on February 12, 1937. It pulls nine coaches but no mail or express cars. *Robert Kennedy, Jr.*

the Clay Center Branch between Belleville, Kansas, and a connection and trackage rights over the SP from McFarland, Kansas, to Kansas City.

It seemed inevitable and logical that, if sale by dismemberment occurred, the SP would get the line from Tucumcari east. Going a step further: should we be able to buy the portion of the bankrupt road we wanted, a line owned and/or controlled by the Grande would be required from Kansas City to St. Louis and one from Council Bluffs, Iowa, to Chicago.

The Milwaukee was in somewhat of a shaky condition, and there were rumors the IC would apply for a merger with the GM&O. The Milwaukee could provide a line to Chicago and the GM&O to St. Louis, in addition to becoming a secondary route to Chicago.

MILWAUKEE EYES LINES

Upon being approached, the Milwaukee readily agreed to talk. H.T. (Hal) Benson and I met with Milwaukee management at Union Station, Chicago, January 31, 1972. These people were the first we had had contact with who unreservedly cooperated and gave me carte blanche to go anywhere on their railroad and to ask for any figures or information I desired. The reception given Hal and I was almost too good to be true. In a session the following day, the stinger was applied. They wanted us to look at all the CMStP&P lines east of Council Bluffs, north to Milwaukee then west to Aberdeen and Mobridge, Wisconsin.

This was some package to open and evaluate the contents, and it was winter. During the following 2 1/2 to 3 months I covered a great deal of the Midwest north of Council Bluffs and west to Mobridge, South Dakota. This included all the major Milwaukee main lines and some branches. Never at any time did the Milwaukee fail to be good hosts.

Much of this territory also contained a number of Rock Island lines and branches. I took advantage of this and combined the Milwaukee investigation with Rock Island inspections.

As a connection from Council Bluffs the Milwaukee was an excellent opportunity, but as for the whole railroad purchase, "No thanks." Milwaukee had not gone the route that Rock Island had, but there was a significant amount of deferred maintenance.

GRASS RAILS

On both the Milwaukee and Rock Island in Iowa, and parts of Minnesota and Nebraska, a number of the virtually unused short branches and spurs presented an unusual feature. On the rare occasions when a train operated on them it was literally *running on grass*. This grass was peculiar to the area. It was pratically evergreen, rapid growing, luxuriant and having a heavy, matted

This photograph and the two below, display the superb bridgework and maintenance on the Gulf, Mobile & Ohio. *John Norwood*

178

This is a trackside view of the station at Roodhouse, Illinois on April 11, 1972—one track side, that is, for this building is set in the triangle formed by the St. Louis route and the Chicago route. *M.D. McCarter collection*

root system that was impervious to any sprays or digging out. The rails were buried under the mat. In many instances they could not be seen except in cases where an engine and cars had run on them recently. Becoming curious as to what was under the grass, I obtained a spade and cut out sections of sod between the rails at several random locations.

Uniformly the ties showed advanced decay with grass roots growing into and around the rotted wood. The base and web of the rails were encased so tightly in the strong, tenacious roots they were held sufficiently in place for lightweight engines to run safely over them at slow speed.

The IC-GM&O contemplated merger was gaining momentum, and the Rio Grande tried to get in on the action. The Rio Grande thought that the portion desired could be a route to St. Louis and a secondary one to Chicago. Division of the routes was at Roodhouse, Illinois.

Summer had come by the time I went to the GM&O. For a couple years I had been working alone on the Rock Island follow-up, and the Milwaukee. I worked alone on the GM&O. We did not have official sanction from the GM&O to be making this study. However, as earlier learned on the Rock Island, station and road forces were antipathetic to the IC. All the relevant information needed was readily available without assistance from railroad officers. Aside from the muggy

atmosphere, myriads of insects and a few snake scares in the river bottoms, it was an enjoyable six weeks along the GM&O.

For some inexplicable reason our Traffic Department had asked me to make cursory examination of the Monon from Louisville, Kentucky, to the Chicago area including Gary and Hammond, Indiana. Three or four days were spent doing this. I did not then, or later, develop any rationale for this request. There simply was nothing of interest on the Monon.

CURSED CATFISH

During the years and on several thousand of miles of railroads out in the boondocks, I had never suffered any illness. Those few days on the Monon broke the charm. Near a small town in southern Indiana I had the evening meal in an almost perfect setting at a superb restaurant. The freshly caught catfish were prepared absolutely to perfection as were the hushpuppies and side dishes. Unfortunately, the catfish were contaminated. I tied up for the night at a small town. About midnight I awakened with unbearable stomach cramps and diarrhea. There was no doctor in the town but the next morning an old dried up druggist mixed up a brew for me that was almost worse than the affliction. Whatever was in the concoction, however, it worked.

The GM&O employees were not the only ones antagonistic to an Illinois Central takeover. Its

179

Gulf, Mobile & Ohio Engine No. 748 leaves Creve Coeur, Illinois on September 10, 1978. *M.D. McCarter collection*

president and management, having at some point in the past divined the IC would be after them, instituted a program designed to use up all the surplus money they had. The program consisted of much bridge and roadway work, station and equipment refurbishing.

Without doubt, that portion of the GM&O was the sweetest piece of railroad I had ever seen up to that date and since. The entire line and plant looked like it had just had the "last spike" driven and was ready for the first train.

MERGER CASE RULED

Back on the Rio Grande I did not have time to make a detailed report before the ICC ruled that because the Grande did not have an actual, physical connection with the GM&O, it was not eligible to enter the IC-GM&O merger case. The KCS was already in but had not made the exhaustive study I had. The KCS and Rio Grande were on very friendly terms at that period. I was loaned, along with data, to the KCS to assist them in preparing their case and at the hearing. The merger was approved.

Having suffered through a decade of merger mania, railroads were sick of them and anything relating to them. During this decade I had been privileged to see and be involved on more miles of railroad than the most dedicated railfan could ever

dream of. Under the best president any railroad ever had, I had freedom to operate as I desired and enjoyed his confidence. He also never questioned my expense accounts, although admittedly I lived well while on the road. And, when required to elicit information, I entertained appropriate railroad people right up to the point of not being ostentatious.

MY RETIREMENT

Relegated to an office job again, the four walls just kept squeezing tighter and tighter. Routine and relatively unimportant work was driving me up the wall. In February, 1975, I took an early retirement. At a retirement party I publicly took oath I would never again get in sight, hearing or smell of a railroad.

How naive can a mature man be? Once infected by the virus of the railroad bug, there is no cure. Once the infective agent is in your blood stream, you are a goner, past recovery.

The Lord knows I tried to keep my word. For about three years my wife and I saw a lot of the world. But there were railroads in Germany, Switzerland, Italy, Mexico and Alaska. That bug and its virus became active again every time I saw or rode on one. I did have enough resistance to turn down the offer of a job with the Terminal Railroad Association at St. Louis.

These coupled Gulf, Mobile & Ohio Units No. 724 and 725 pass Roodhouse, Illinois on April 8, 1971. *M.D. McCarter collection*

People still several years away from retirement will not credit the next statement. Traveling just for pleasure and to fulfill pre-retirement ambitions can become deathly boring. At least, this proved true for me and my wife.

CONSULTING AGAIN

When I was approached by R.L. Banks and Associates and one other group of lawyers in Washington, D.C. to act as an independent consultant and work with them on pending railroad abandonment cases, I eagerly accepted. Frankly, I would have worked for expense money only, but I did not have to. Consulting is very lucrative employment. Then it was fun to be appearing as the opposition to railroads wanting to abandon pieces of track. They were still making their presentations on the same premises used since the first abandonment case was heard. These were valid statistics and premises based on ICC rules of accounting that had not been changed for 50 years. But they overlooked the fact there was a new breed of examiners hearing the cases. They were delving into the impact on communities and people. Statistics, they knew, under ICC regulations could be only a tenuous smoke screen and a misrepresentation.

All-weather highways were being built like a spider web across the country. Truck capacity,

speed and availability had reached a point where people and communities did not give a hoot whether they had a railroad or not. Railroads could apply for an abandonment and be almost certain there would be no opposition. Consultants and expert witnesses in railroad matters were out of work.

Before I had to store my traveling bags, however, I had a chance to again be on the Milwaukee a long way from Chicago. Milwaukee petitioned to abandon the branch from Newport, Washington, to Metaline Falls, in the same state. Newport Port Authority opposed and hired me.

Because of the devastation caused by hurricane Hazel the SP wanted to abandon the San Diego & Arizona Eastern. The San Diego Port Authority, Sonora & Baja California RR (Mexican), and numerous others were opposed. I was employed by the Port Authority. There were others, but the SD&AE was the most memorable. In all of these cases my employment was with R.L. Banks or a similar group of attorneys and accountants.

My vow of severance from all things pertaining to railroads was so much idle talk, but to this day I have never ridden Amtrak, the Cumbres and Toltec Scenic, nor the privately owned present Durango and Silverton Railroad. And, I do not intend to.

This weathered Gulf, Mobile & Ohio Engine No. 55 waits at Dwight, Illinois on May 1, 1971. *M.D. McCarter collection*

This is a quiet moment at the Atchison, Topeka & Santa Fe-Illinois Central Gulf-Mobile & Ohio Tower at Chicago-Corwith yard, May 1, 1971. *M.D. McCarter collection*

This is the view passenger train patrons enjoyed as they entered Chicago Union Station on July 14, 1972. *M.D. McCarter collection*

Epilogue

Some Dreams Come True — Some Don't

A philosopher named Blount wrote, "As dreams are the fancies of those that sleep, so fancies are but the dreams of those awake."

I have had some wonderful dreams while sleeping and more while wide awake that were wilder and more fantastic. None of the sleeping dreams came true, but many of the daydreams have.

The earliest of these dreamed along the tracks of the Kansas City Southern almost three score and 10 years ago was of being the engineer on a high rolling steamer on the point of a string of varnish and making the hills echo with its whistle. And, to sit in the diner of that string of cars, as part of the group of rich diners seated at linen-clothed tables with their settings of silver and crystal.

I also dreamed of being present when two trains collided, and wondered what it would be like—the sounds and the chaos.

DREAMS FULFILLED

Over the years, in some form, these fancies have come true. I have sat on the right hand side of a narrow gauge "sport model" locomotive and the more powerful tonnage hauling K-37 class engine of the Rio Grande's narrow gauge. I have known the feeling of power at the throttle of one of the Grande's EMD F-7s rolling eastward at sunrise across the Utah desert.

To be honest about it, always on these occasions there was a nervous engine driver at my side telling me what to do and when to do it. I gave up trying to fire an engine up Cumbres Pass when the engineman and fireboy became exasperated with me for not keeping the needle against the peg and requested of me, not politely, to get the hell out of the way. I was finally convinced the thrill of being at the throttle was not worth the worry I caused the legitimate hoghead by being there.

This was brought sharply home when, on one occasion, I was told, "Get your butt out of my seat. I don't want you there when we tip over the grade going down the big curve to the bridge over Green River. You can blow the whistle for the station and crossing if you want to do something."

So there went my dream of being a trainmaster who could also fire an engine or handle a throttle. But it did strengthen a fact of life of being a boss. Those performing work under your supervision dislike you trying to be helpful. A boss just ain't appreciated by nobody.

On November 11, 1954 one of the biggest wrecks on the Rio Grande occurred at the Green River bridge caused by a burnt off journal giving way just after going around the big curve almost at the station location. I was trainmaster then and spent a week at Green River in the cleanup.

The part of the dream of wining and dining at a table set with heavy silver and crystal did come true. As an officer I frequently had this experience on the *California Zephyr*, the acme of luxurious railroad diners. There were other diners I patronized on other railroads, but none closely approached the atmosphere on the *California Zephyr*.

TRAIN COLLISION

The wondering about what a collision between two engines or trains would be like was brought to reality while I was trainmaster of the Alamosa Division. Nat Holt was filming the picture *Denver & Rio Grande* using the Silverton Branch for most of the locale. Along with T.J. Cummins, I was assigned to work with Holt while the filming was in progress.

One scene in the story was to be of two locomotives in a head-on collision. A location was selected on the Silverton Branch between Tefft and Tacoma where there was a flat area large enough to set up for the picture. There a piece of track of sufficient length was laid adjacent to the operative track. It was designed and built to be absolutely straight and perfectly level.

Two C-class engines due to be scrapped but still operative were sold to Holt and moved to the location. There they were checked over, and the front interior of each engine was loaded with old journal oil, magnesium, gun powder and dynamite. Each engine was provided with a protruding rod so arranged and aligned they would come in contact and set off detonators to the explosive and smoke material in the engines.

On the day of the shoot the engines were steamed up and manned by two Rio Grande employees. The engines were spaced at the ends of the short track. On a signal from the cameramen the engines were put in motion at the same time, and the enginemen jumped off and ran to prepared safety pits.

The engines raced at each other, and the detonating rams made contact perfectly. Noise of the collision and explosives going off was tremendous. Billows of black smoke enveloped the engines. It was a very impressive scene and a real collision instead of the usual scene produced by running an engine through a large mirror.

And I was there to help set it up, watch and

hear it. A speculation that began about 30 years earlier along the KCS railroad in northeastern Oklahoma had been brought to a final conclusion.

Sitting there under a shady tree near the KCS tracks watching the *Flying Crow* wheel by, how I envied all those rich folks on it and wished I was grown up and could join them. Well, due to the mania for railroad mergers in the 60s and being assigned to being a major participant in the Rio Grande's role in the mergers, I was privileged to join them. Very soon, however, I had to admit that my plebeian tastes found more pleasure and satisfaction from beer than from champagne: John Bushmill Whiskey as opposed to aged wines and brandy; cornbread and beans instead of filet mignon. I have to be honest. While on the 10 years of this assignment, and later as an independent consultant and having an almost unlimited expense account, I did not resist living it up, although I did draw the line at caviar.

During that period it was enlightening, sometimes pleasurably, and often very much the opposite, hobnobbing and being privy with prominent and important people. There were governors, ICC commissioners, state utility representatives, heads of large railroads and major industry transportation heads. Frequently in the assignments I was involved in situations where ethics and morality were made necessarily complex, and often cynical, decisions were made. No two cases or incidents were alike. Sometimes the decision to "do it" or "not to do it" could be made at the moment; other times it required deeper consideration and soul searching.

ELEANOR ROOSEVELT

One of the most memorable incidents was the pleasure and privilege of spending an hour or more with Eleanor Roosevelt. What a woman she was. It was unfortunate she did not photograph well for, in truth, she was a very attractive woman.

There is a bit of the sadist in all of us. There is no one who at some time has not wished they were in a position to make an authority figure squirm or suffer to humiliate him. I was able, while appearing as a witness at merger hearings, to give my sadistic streak free rein for my own pleasure at the instigation of our lawyers. For I found, as did our lawyers, that I had the ability to obfuscate my answer to questions from opposing attorneys to the point they were climbing the walls, without antagonizing the ICC or state utilities examiners. There was an almost sensual pleasure derived from watching a $1 million legal eagle become more confused and frustrated by my answers because he was unversed in railroad terminology or technology. I took pains to be very sure that my answers were correct and clear to persons knowledgeable about railroads.

There was, and is, a lot of satisfaction in knowing I was privileged to be active in the center of a phase of railroad history in the making.

GROWNUP DREAMS

Part of growing up is the making and losing of fancies as maturity is approached. Some dreams come true — some do not and most often it is just as well that they do not. During the Great Depression when there was no family money to let me finish high school, my father and one other old retired telegrapher literally beat the Morse code into my brain in lieu of schooling. I became determined that the one thing I would never be was a railroader. So much for determination. In 1937, due to financial and family circumstances, I started railroading.

For eight wonderful years prior to that the world was my oyster. I was young and fancy free. And, I do mean fancy free. There was a series of fancies and ambitions for the future.

There was a phase of working for ranchers, cattle and sheepmen, when I was going to be a sheep or cattle baron, then a short stint of working at a sawmill to become a lumber king, followed by work in coal and hard rock mines, and the dream of becoming a great mining capitalist.

A summer of being part of a surveying crew along the ridge of the San Juan mountains using packhorses and canvas tents was immediately followed by a winter of trapping destructive beavers on a rich man's 83,000 acre private recreational portion of an isolated valley at the head of the Navajo River in Colorado. It was so isolated I spent a total of 97 days without having contact with another human in the wilderness of snow, mountains and river at an elevation of about 9,000 feet.

During that three months of solitude I dreamed of going to Alaska to have my own cabin and trap line where I would harvest a fortune in silver fox furs and live on moose meat and fish from the richly stocked lakes and streams. That dream filled my mind during the days.

At night, the dreams were somewhat different. Dreams of Jean Harlow, Ginger Rogers, Lana Turner, Rita Hayworth and Dolores del Rio. In the spring a young man's thoughts turn to love, so they say, but from my experience I think this is more true in the winter if you are young and alone in a snow-covered world.

In the spring, instead of going to Hollywood, I went to Texas and worked as a tool dresser on oil drilling rigs. But I missed the mountains and returned to Colorado.

Less than a week after returning I signed on with the Bureau of Reclamation as an axeman. The project was making a survey for the Transmountain Water Project, a proposal to make use of water resources of the Rio Grande, San Juan,

An eastbound caboose hop carries white signals at Hanging Bridge on the Arkansas River. *Colorado State Historical Society*

Navajo, Blanco, Animas and Chama rivers. The position of axeman was short-lived. I was boosted up to chainman-rodman on a land survey portion of the team.

The project engineer in charge decided I had experience in mining (I maybe stretched that experience a bit) and enough practical knowledge of geology to qualify for the job of field geologist on the project.

Another fancy came full circle. I would become another Herbert Hoover and roam the world geologizing and supervising the development of great mineral discoveries. Anyway, for a couple of years I dreamed. Then, because I did not have a degree in geology, I was informed that if I wanted to con-

tinue with the Bureau of Reclamation I would have to take a leave of absence for a year and attend a school that would give me a quickie diploma and degree. There used to be such schools and maybe there still are.

I could not do it. I had met a young lady I thought had all the attributes of Jean, Ginger, Lana, Rita and Dolores in one. We married, and at the time the Bureau gave me the ultimatum, had our first child, a son. I had to quit dreaming of being a later Herbert Hoover. The young lady has been with me 58 years and has kept me from dreaming or thinking of all the sexpots who peopled my dreams during three months of snow and solitude at the head of the Navajo River.

Bathing the Behemoths—
One Last Story

The three lowliest jobs on a railroad in the days of steam were the coal chute mucker, the cinderpit man and the engine wiper, or swipers. Yet each was as vital to efficient operation as the highest paid brass hat.

The coal chute must always be full; the cinderpit must always be ready to accept the next dumping; and the underpinning of the engines must always be clean enough for the machinist to be able to make a thorough inspection for flaws in any part.

Consider that each of these heavy, vital parts

were cast of molten metal, run into patterns formed in green casting sand structured around wooden replicas. Pattern making was a profession in itself. After the Rio Grande was entirely dieselized, carloads of these works of art were carted to the dump yard.

After the vital mechanisms were thoroughly cleaned, the machinist first gave them a hammer test to see if there were any out-of-tune sounds. Then the tightness of fit of driver wheel tire to wheel was tested using a thin, sharp gauge making a circuit around the joint. The flange was then

The tires, flanges, wheel cores, pins and rods of the behemoths of steam engine days got a lot more baths than the men who did the cleaning. It was a dirty, hot job. Today's EPA would have a heyday. Just think of all the grease and sand that hot stream of water washed off the surfaces into a drain which then flowed into nearby rivers or open sumps where it soaked into the subsurface or evaporated into the atmosphere. The bath had a more important reason for being done than an aesthetic one. These particular parts of an engine had to be squeaky clean so that inspections for cracks, folds and crevices could reveal any and all flaws. The inherent pounding of the wheel against the rail as the eccentrics turned them was conducive to producing metal fatigue. *Norm Schreiner collection*

calipered for wear and given a feel test for nicks or wear. Each rod pin and journal was tested for trueness and freedom from any off center conditions that would cause vibration or excessive wear. Lubricating fuel channels were tested to be sure they were open, and the supply of lubricant moved properly through them.

Running gear inspection and maintenance for diesel engines is much simpler, for the movement of the drive wheel is continuous. Conversely the driver of a steam engine, at the instant the eccentric changes the direction of thrust, receives a short hammerlike blow. Upon the expertise and thoroughness of the machinist rests the safe operation of a steam engine.

The first emergence of the women's rights movement may be said to have started during World War I. With so many men in service, railroads began to recruit women capable of doing the work of engine wiping and cleaning. Such women usually were sturdy, and were often Irish, Scandinavian or African-American girls with a farm background. They performed superbly, and after the war could see no reason why they should not retain jobs that had previously been given men. So the battle for women's rights may have begun.

We had one on the Alamosa Division who was a legend in her own time. She worked as a wiper in the Durango roundhouse throughout the war, then took courses to learn secretarial and stenographic work. Upon graduation she was given a job as the clerk of a trainmaster then located at Durango. When this position was abolished she moved to Division headquarters at Alamosa in the Superintendent's office.

When I knew her while I was Chief Dispatcher there, she was close to 70 years old and refused to retire under the railroad retirement act provisions. She was not pushed to do so because she was a grand old gal and extremely competent. She had not missed a day's work in years. One day she did not show up on time or later in the day. Worried, the Superintendent sent someone to check on her. She was found in the bathroom of her home in the same erect position she sat at her desk. Her great old heart had failed, and she passed over into the Valhalla of all good railroaders.

BIBLIOGRAPHY

Robert G. Athearn, 1962
Rebel of the Rockies

Lucius Beebe
Bulletin No. 67A, Narrow Gauge Railroads of Colorado

Herbert O. Brayer, 1949
Early Financing of the Denver and Rio Grande Railway

Keith L. Bryant, Jr., 1982
Atchison, Topeka & Santa Fe Railway

Colorado Geological Survey
Bulletins Nos. 1 to 6, inclusive

Colorado Historical Society, 1986
The Georgetown Loop

George A. Crofutt, 1966
Crofutt's Guide of Colorado (Cubar Associates reprint)

Denver and Rio Grande Summaries of Equipment
Various Years

Denver and Rio Grande RR System, 1916
Official Roster No. 10

Denver and Rio Grande Western, 1923
Official Roster No. 11

Perry Eberhart, 1959
Guide to Colorado Ghost Towns

Vardis Fisher and Opal Laurel Holmes, 1968
Gold Rushes and Mining Camps of the Early American West

Leroy R. Hafen, 1948
Colorado and Its People, Vols. 1 and 2

Donald Heimburger, 1981
Rio Grande Steam Locomotives, Standard Gauge

Rossiter Johnson, 1967
Campfires and Battlefields (Civil War)

Railway Guides
Various editions

Marshall Sprague, 1964
The Great Gates

Jackson C. Thode, 1972
A Century of Passenger Trains

Frances Toor, 1966
New Guide to Mexico

True West Magazine
Issue of August, 1988

Carl Ubbelohde, 1965
A Colorado History

John Hoyt Williams, 1988
A Great and Shining Road

And numerous reference books, files and archives at the Colorado State Historical Society and the Denver Public Library.

INDEX